WILDERNESS SURVIVAL SKILLS

BOB HOLTZMAN

WILDERNESS SURVIVAL SKILLS

HOW TO STAY ALIVE IN THE WILD WITH JUST A BLADE & YOUR WITS

BOB HOLTZMAN

CHARTWELL
BOOKS

© 2012 by Quid Publishing

Conceived, designed, and produced by
Quid Publishing
Level 4 Sheridan House
114 Western Road
Hove BN3 1DD

www.quidpublishing.com

This edition published in 2012 by
CHARTWELL BOOKS
an imprint of BOOK SALES
a division of Quarto Publishing Group USA Inc.
276 Fifth Avenue Suite 206
New York, New York 10001
USA

ISBN-13: 978-0-7858-2875-4

Printed in China

Reprinted 2013, 2014

3 5 7 9 10 8 6 4

Thanks to survival experts Michael Pewtherer and Rich Johnson, who taught me much of what I am now able to impart to others on the subject, and with whom working was a pleasure. Thanks also to Mors Kochanski, with whom I have not had the pleasure, but from whose writings on knives and axes I have gratefully extracted much wisdom. I appreciate the help of Ronald Anderson at Owls Head Transportation Museum and the use of that fine institution's machine shop. Special gratitude to Greg Rössel, who allowed me to push him around for an afternoon, never once taking advantage of the edge tools I placed at his disposal.

To Cate, who encourages, comforts, and makes life fun: thank you for making this book and so much else possible.

CONTENTS

INTRODUCTION: WOULD YOU MAKE IT OUT ALIVE?

The habit of being prepared for emergencies is one that comes naturally to some and remains foreign to others. Some people keep their eyes open for trouble, do their best to avoid it, and, if they can't, either know how to confront it, or are at least ready to make the attempt with the knowledge and tools at their disposal. Others—the ones whom trouble takes entirely by surprise—more often succumb to dangers because they have both failed to anticipate them and have failed to instill in themselves a well-grounded belief in their own competence to deal with emergencies.

This book is for both groups—those who acknowledge the potential dangers of wilderness and wish to be better prepared to meet them, and those who wish to learn about those dangers as the first step toward adopting a habit of preparedness. Once established, this habit applies to any situation, be it wilderness or city, natural or social, a cliff face or a work place. Then it is only the specifics of the situation that must be learned.

This book addresses the dangers of wilderness and appropriate responses to those dangers. It is based on a simple premise, stated as a question: How would you survive if you were lost or stranded in the wilderness with only a knife?

This premise isn't as artificial as it may seem, and most wilderness travelers can envision scenarios in which it might arise: a canoeing expedition in which boat and gear are lost in rapids; a trekking horse that stumbles into a steep canyon, again with all the gear; a float plane accident from which you barely escape.

Even if these scenarios are unlikely, the premise is still a valuable one, for a knife is an all-purpose survival tool, capable of meeting almost any need. Master knife skills and your ability to cope with any wilderness challenge is vastly improved, regardless of what other tools you may possess.

The second premise—what if you also had an axe?—is no less instructive. If you lose all your gear, you will probably lose your axe too, since few people—even wilderness travelers—carry an axe on their belt at all times. But axes are often carried into the wilderness, where they are capable of performing many tasks that are difficult or impossible with knives. It only makes sense, therefore, to include this other common edge tool in the discussion.

WHAT DO WE MEAN BY "WILDERNESS?"

Wilderness can be any natural area greatly distant from man. For the purpose of this book, we generally mean woodland wilderness, areas of abundant trees and often undergrowth. On occasion, we include desert environments where some trees or other plant resources are available. This focus was chosen because these are the most common settings for wilderness work and recreation, and because knives and axes are useful tools in these environments. The polar ice cap is just as much a wilderness as any boreal forest, but if you are stranded there with nothing but a knife, you are probably not going to make it. Sorry. There's only so much you can make with a block of ice, and a fire isn't among them.

WHAT DO WE MEAN BY "SURVIVAL?"

Survival is a continuum—an ongoing series of incidents that must be addressed. Some of them require a rapid response. If caught in a winter storm, for example, one must build shelter and make fire quickly in order to survive the night. Other incidents have longer time horizons. Having survived the night, you may need to feed yourself for several weeks.

Survival, then, can mean different things and include different outcomes. You may be entirely fit and know exactly where you are, and need only live through a brutally cold night before you can hike out to safety the following day. Or you may be hundreds of miles from the nearest habitation with no one knowing your whereabouts—in which case, survival might mean living off the land for days or weeks before you reach help. Or movement may be unwise or impossible—you may be totally lost, stranded, or forced to stay put because of an injury in your party—and survival then means maintaining yourselves in one place for an indefinite period while you await rescue.

No matter what the challenge, duration, or objective, the skills in this book are meant to help you survive.

SKILLS BEYOND THE WILDERNESS, AND THE MACHO FALLACY

We hope that you never find your life in danger out in the wilds. But even though true survival emergencies are rare, we can almost guarantee that you will use many of the skills in this book, whether you venture into the wilderness or not. Selecting a good knife and keeping it sharp have everyday utility in the home as well as in the woods. Knowing how to carve and chop safely can help you avoid injury any time you use a knife or axe.

TIP

Elements of this book are not in accordance with good environmental practices, and are intended for emergencies, where minor damage to the environment is considered an acceptable compromise.

We've tried to be realistic and practical throughout, and have avoided giving advice that might encourage you to enter dangerous situations. Too many people—men especially, unfortunately—treat dangerous weapons as extensions of their personalities, and for many, an interest in "self-defense" is really a veiled wish for an opportunity to commit self-justified mayhem.

A big knife makes you not a shred more competent or worthy of respect. A knife is just a tool—an immensely useful one that could save your life, but just a tool nonetheless. Treat it as any good carpenter treats his tools—with care and respect, using them only for their proper purposes—and your knife will serve you well and keep you out of trouble.

CHOOSING A KNIFE

ASSESSING YOUR NEEDS

Choosing a knife could be one of the most important decisions you make before heading into the wilderness. The right knife can make almost everything you do easier, from preparing your next meal to helping yourself out of a life-threatening situation. In fact, choosing a knife might be two or three of the most important decisions you'll make, because no one knife can do everything well, and you may want to pack a backup or two.

WHAT YOU CAN DO WITH A KNIFE

With a bewildering variety of knives available, the place to start is understanding what kind of work your knife or knives might be called upon to do. The knife has a role to play in most of the primary tasks of wilderness survival.

Shelter

Protecting yourself from the elements is among the highest priorities. You might starve to death in three weeks, and die of dehydration in three days. But in the wrong weather without shelter, you could die of exposure in just three hours.

A really rugged knife, with a blade of 3" (8cm) or more, is capable of cutting limbs and saplings and stripping bark to make an emergency shelter. If you're not equipped with yards of string or rope, a knife can be used to harvest certain plants and extract from them fibers from which to make the cordage required for shelter construction.

Fire

While fires can often be made and maintained with small twigs and dead stuff that is easily broken by hand, a rugged knife can make wood gathering and fire building much more efficient. Additionally, fire-making tools can be produced with knives.

Food

Food is plentiful in many wilderness environments. A small pocket knife is sufficient for most food-gathering tasks, although when hunting game, a larger fixed-blade knife tends to be more useful either in its own right, or to create other hunting tools. Certain traps and snares can be easily created with a small knife, while larger knives are handier for others. Some knives work better

A very small pocket knife will suffice for cutting bandages, making slings, and making small incisions.

than others for skinning and dressing game. While any knife can be used to clean a fish, a fishing knife makes the job easier.

Water

Aside from its use for carving a digging stick, a knife will not be much help in securing drinking water.

Navigation and Transportation

A knife isn't much help in finding your way. A few knives have small magnetic compasses built in, but these are usually just novelties, rarely accurate enough for navigating over land. Should you need to cross a body of water, however, various types of watercraft can be built in the field with knives of different sizes and capabilities.

THE UNEXPECTED

By its nature, finding yourself in a survival situation means that things have not gone according to plan, and certain of your expectations have been confounded. Maybe you need to fix a broken backpack, restitch a hiking boot, or remove a fishhook that's embedded in your calf muscle. The trusty Swiss Army Knife, or its steroidal younger cousin the multi-tool may provide just the tool for the job. You literally never know whether an awl, screwdriver, magnifying glass, wire cutter, pliers, scissors, or even a tiny LED flashlight might save the day. And there's no telling how many wilderness expeditions have been saved from disappointment, if not disaster, by the corkscrew on a Swiss Army Knife.

Signaling

A large, sturdy knife can be used to produce certain signaling devices that might enable you to signal for help over long distances—for example, from one mountain peak to another, or from the ground to a search plane overhead.

FIXED-BLADE OR FOLDING?

All knives fall into one of two categories: fixed-blade or folding. Fixed-blade knives tend to excel at certain tasks, while folders have clear advantages in other situations. Although you may form a clear preference, neither is "better," so it's important to recognize the respective advantages of both kinds. Rather than choosing between them, it is highly desirable to bring at least one of each into the wilderness, using whichever is better suited to the task at hand.

PROS AND CONS

Other things being equal, fixed-blade knives are sturdier, less prone to failure, and capable of performing heavier work. Also known as sheath knives, fixed-blade knives are quicker and easier to deploy, and safer to the extent that there is no hinge to fail, so they can't fold up inadvertently on your hand.

Folding knives are more compact, and are easier and safer to carry. Many have more than one blade or multiple tools, providing more functions than a fixed-blade knife. Although the two types overlap in size over most of their ranges, the largest outdoor

knives tend to have fixed blades, and the smallest tend to be folders.

But "other things" are rarely equal. Well-made folding knives may be sturdier and more durable than bargain-priced sheath knives. Some folders have special features that make them quick and easy to deploy, while a poorly designed sheath can inhibit access to a fixed-blade knife. Some so-called "survival knives" of the fixed-blade variety have a number of built-in tools, while many folders offer only a single blade.

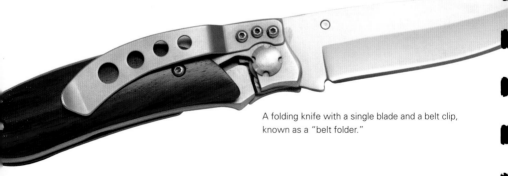

A folding knife with a single blade and a belt clip, known as a "belt folder."

POCKET KNIFE TERMINOLOGY

SHEATH KNIFE TERMINOLOGY

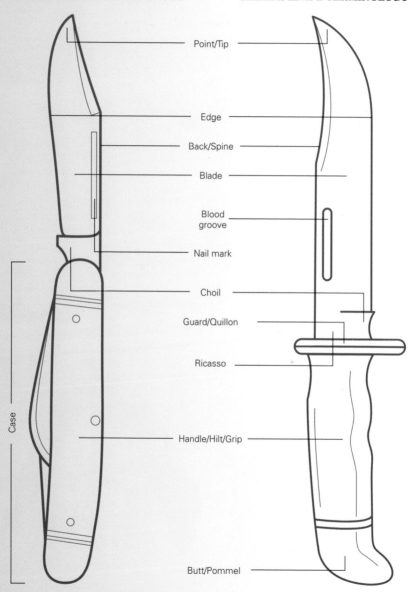

Point/Tip

Edge

Back/Spine

Blade

Blood groove

Nail mark

Choil

Guard/Quillon

Ricasso

Handle/Hilt/Grip

Case

Butt/Pommel

MAIN CHOICES

Your main survival knives should almost certainly be one or more of the following types: a standard sheath knife; a pocket knife; or a belt folder. (The latter two categories are both folding knives.) Consider packing in addition some of the more specialized types discussed later.

1 **Sheath Knife**

One of mankind's first and most basic tools, the fixed-blade knife remains among the most useful. It is so elemental that it scarcely requires description, and it is subject to endless refinements of form, material, and workmanship.

In essence, a fixed-blade knife is a blade with a handle attached for a secure and comfortable grip. Different blade shapes work better for different tasks—for example, carving or splitting wood, skinning and butchering game, scaling and filleting fish, cutting rope or tree limbs. Different handles may be more durable, more comfortable, or offer a better grip than others. The design of the tang—the part of the blade hidden within the handle—plays an important role in determining the knife's strength.

Every fixed-blade outdoors knife requires a sheath to protect the blade from damage and to enable the user to carry it safely.

2 **Belt Folder**

The belt folder is often the most basic version of the folding knife: a single blade that folds into a slot in the handle. Although this configuration shortens the knife when it's not in use and protects the edge from damage, the belt folder is too large (typically at least 3.5", or 9cm long when folded) to carry comfortably in a trouser pocket. Instead, it is carried in a sheath on a belt. As with all folding knives, the tang is merely a stub, drilled to accept a hinge pin on which the blade pivots. Although a single blade is the most common, some belt folders are equipped with two. Tools other than cutting blades are less common.

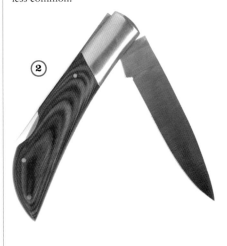

①

②

MULTI-TOOLS

Although often lumped in with knives, a multi-tool is in fact a different animal—a multi-purpose tool that almost always includes a knife blade along with several other implements. Most feature pliers/wire cutters as the primary tool, with some combination of flat and cross-head (Phillips) screwdrivers, wrenches, wire strippers, scissors, saws, files, can openers, and other tools being offered in a variety of models. The entire device typically folds into a compact steel rectangle, with the various tools hidden inside the handle. Because of the compromises inherent in such a design, multi-tools tend to be less convenient as knives, per se, than a conventional pocket knife. That said, they tend to be of high quality and offer a great deal of convenience in many situations.

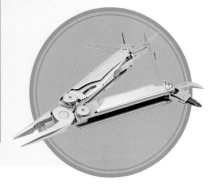

③ Pocket Knife

Usually 3" (8cm) or under in length when closed, the pocket knife can be as simple as a belt folder or, as in the well-known Swiss Army Knife, it can boast a multiplicity of blades and other tools ranging from saws, screwdrivers, and awls to LED flashlights, toothpicks, and computer flash drives. Obviously, some of these implements are more useful in wilderness survival situations than others.

LOCKBACKS

A lockback is a feature that may apply to any folding knife, in which the blade locks into position when open—usually automatically—to prevent the possibility of it accidentally closing on the user's hand. The blade must be unlocked in order to close the knife, and on many designs this is awkward to perform one-handed. Many belt folders are lockbacks. Some pocket knives have a lock on their largest blade, but rarely on smaller blades or other tools.

BLADE SHAPE

A lot depends upon the shape of the blade. Blades differ in both profile and cross-section, and both influence how well a knife will work for different purposes. Along with the quality of the steel, the cross-section shape also limits how sharp the blade can be, and how well it will hold that edge. The shape of the blade will also affect your choice of sharpening equipment, your sharpening techniques, and how often you have to use them.

PROFILE OR PATTERN
The most obvious aspect of a blade's shape is its profile or pattern—its shape in silhouette. Out of the hundreds of different knife profiles in use around the world, just a few comprise logical options for general wilderness use. Almost every knife you find in an outdoor goods store will feature one of these patterns.

"Normal" Blade
The favorite of many outdoors experts, the "normal" blade has a straight spine and a curved edge. The point is fine enough to carve holes. No part of the blade is higher than the point, which thus clears the way for easy penetration of the entire blade when thrusting. The straight spine, if sufficiently robust, is good for pounding on with a baton (a club). The gently curved blade allows for

good carving control while providing a longer cutting edge than a straight blade.

Curved, Trailing-Point Blade
A lightweight design, best for slicing and slashing. Narrow from edge to spine, it is not as strong as a "normal" blade. Although the narrow point is good for fine work, it is not so good for forceful thrusting, because the point has nothing directly behind it and may even be higher than the handle.

Clip-Point Blade

On this blade type, the tip end of the spine has been "clipped" away to reduce weight and produce a finer point. This allows it to perform like a curved, trailing-point blade toward the tip—good for slicing and skinning—and like a "normal" blade toward the handle—good for heavy work like chopping wood and cutting through bone joints. Although the narrow point may be delicate, it encourages a well-directed penetrating thrust because it is not higher

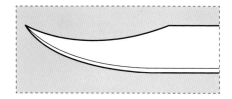

than the handle, as on a curved, trailing-point blade. This is the pattern of the famous Bowie knife, one of the most popular styles of hunting knife.

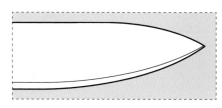

Drop-Point Blade

The curved edge offers the same benefits as a "normal" blade, making it a good carving knife. The point is coaxial with the handle but, because the spine curves down toward the point, this blade type does not penetrate well on a thrust.

Sheepsfoot Blade

The only blade shown with a straight cutting edge, it has a spine that curves all the way down to the point. The knife can be held by the blade, providing excellent control for scraping or careful work with the fairly broad point. The point does not penetrate well, because the "front" of the blade is the broad spine.

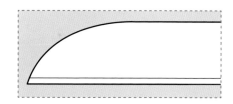

Spear-Point Blade

Although the profile is symmetrical, the blade may or may not be double-edged. Single-edged blades don't penetrate as well, although the height of the point relative to the handle is ideal for thrusting: the two are directly in line with each other. If two-edged, this is the best shape for a penetrating thrust.

GRIND

A blade's cross-section is known as its grind, because during the manufacturing process, metal is removed from the blank by grinding to shape the blade. Almost all knives for outdoor use feature one of the following grinds.

Flat Grind

Both sides of the blade are flat from the edge up to the back. A flat-ground blade can take a very sharp edge, and it is easy to keep sharp in the short run. However, repeated sharpening may change the angle of the edge, and after a while it becomes quite a job to restore the proper angle, because a lot of metal must be removed. (See Chapter 2, on sharpening.)

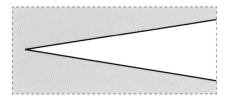

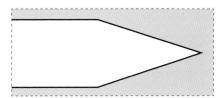

Saber Grind

This is similar to the flat grind, but the ground section extends only partway up the blade, and the rest is parallel-sided. Capable of taking nearly as sharp an edge as a true flat-ground blade, it is easier to maintain over the long run because less metal needs to be removed to maintain the proper edge angle. This style is often called flat-ground.

Hollow Grind

Both sides of the edge are concave. This style can take the sharpest edge, because the two sides of the blade meet at the narrowest angle. This also means it is the most delicate edge, quickly dulled and easily chipped or rolled. Like the other grinds, it can be sharpened with a stone, but if the edge is badly damaged, a sharpening wheel is required to repair it— not something you're likely to be carrying.

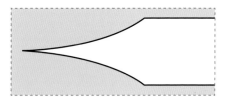

DOUBLE-EDGE BLADES

Leave double-edge blades to martial arts enthusiasts and carnival knife throwers. They have no place in the outdoors. They're more dangerous to the user than single-edge blades, and they're useless for batoning, a tremendously effective technique in which a wooden club is used to strike the spine of the knife to chop through tree limbs and even split small firewood. (See page 63.)

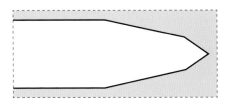

Compound Bevel
Also known as a double bevel, the cutting edge takes a wider angle than the grind above it. This cannot be made as sharp as the other grinds, but the advantage is a tougher, more durable edge that will resist damage and keep its sharpness longer.

Convex Grind
This is the opposite of the hollow grind, with the blade sides convex rather than concave. Also known as a slack-belt grind, because it is produced on an unsupported section of belt between the rollers of a belt grinder, this style offers a good combination of strength and sharpness. Although it cannot be made quite as keen as a hollow- or flat-ground blade, it can take an edge that is sharp enough for anything short of shaving and that will last longer in the field. Although long-term maintenance can be performed with a standard flat stone, it requires more skill than a saber-ground or compound-bevel blade.

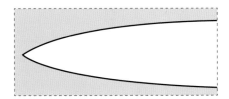

SERRATED AND PLAIN EDGES

Some outdoorspeople have a strong preference for serrated or toothed blades. Many more, it seems, are monogamously attached to a plain edge, and refuse to carry a serrated knife. More practical folk recognize that both have their advantages. Since you'll probably carry more than one knife into the wilderness, why not take at least one of each?

SERRATED BLADES

Paramedics and rescue personnel tend to favor knives with serrated blades, because they cut through nylon webbing and other synthetic fibers more easily. This is great if you need to cut away a car's seat belt to free an accident victim, or maybe cut away the victim's clothing. Many river-rescue experts, who must cut through rope in situations where seconds count, also prefer serrated edges. In general, serrated edges seem to work better on tough, fibrous materials. Some self-defense experts recommend a serrated edge because it cuts flesh more easily, a principle that would apply equally to wild animals as to people.

But let's keep a sense of proportion here. The chances of having to use a knife to defend yourself against either animals or people in the wilderness are vanishingly small, and if killing is really on the agenda, you'll do better using the point of your knife rather than its edge.

PLAIN BLADES

A key advantage of a plain-edge blade is its ease of sharpening. Any sharp knife is better than any dull knife, no matter whether its edge is plain or serrated. A plain edge can be kept sharp with just a few minutes of work, and it requires no special equipment—indeed, you can sharpen a plain-edge blade with almost any rock you pick up in the wild. A serrated blade, in contrast, requires a special tool, and a lot more time and skill. (On the other hand, serrated blades tend to remain sharp longer.) While a plain edge may be somewhat inferior to a serrated one for cutting tough fibers, a sharp plain blade will still cut through rope and webbing and do the job adequately in 99 cases out of 100. It will also do a far better job at many other tasks, such as carving, chopping, and scraping. Where good control and a clean cut are desired, no serrated blade can equal the performance of a sharp plain edge.

COMBINATION BLADES

Since both types of edges have their advantages, many knife makers offer models with blades that combine the two, with a serrated section—almost always closer to the handle—taking up anywhere from a quarter to half of the blade's length, and the remainder being plain. Some users—including some wilderness survival experts—prefer this kind of combination edge. Others feel that, instead of combining the capabilities of the different edges, this hybrid style reduces each by the proportion of the blade length given over to the other type. So a 6" (15cm) blade that's half-serrated is effectively just two 3" (7.5cm) blades, not necessarily in the ideal configuration. Some argue that the plain-edge section should be the one closer to the handle, allowing better control for fine carving tasks.

However, like any plain or serrated edge, any well-made knife with a combination edge has its virtues and its shortcomings, and it's the virtues that will help you survive in the wilderness.

SPECIALTY KNIVES

After you've chosen your primary survival knife or knives, consider adding these to your arsenal for greater convenience or additional functionality.

FISHING KNIFE

Almost every angler keeps a spare pocket knife in his tackle box, but most work gets done with a special-purpose fishing knife. The long, flexible, very narrow blade is made for the delicate work of cleaning (gutting) and filleting, although it may be too delicate to cut effectively through the spinal column of a large fish. Some folding models have a second blade for scaling. This has rounded, dull teeth to work under the scales and lever them out of the skin without cutting the skin itself. Desirable features include handle material that allows you to retain a firm grip even when your hands are coated with blood and slime, and a wrist lanyard to prevent the knife's loss into the water should it slip out of your hand in spite of the handle's "grippiness."

MACHETES AND BUSH KNIVES

A machete typically has a blade at least 12" (30cm) long, and is used with a swinging or chopping stroke. A bush knife is a machete with a brush hook extending from the spine of the blade. Both are too large to be carried casually, but are worth considering if you seriously anticipate having to cut your way through dense brush. Either can serve as a light-duty axe. Some might argue that a machete isn't really a knife, but survival doesn't care much about semantics.

SKINNER

What makes a good skinning knife is a matter of opinion and what you're used to. Knives sold as skinners differ so greatly from one another that it's impossible to make generalizations. Some have long narrow blades; some are short, broad, and leaf-shaped; some have the "normal" profile; and others are classic clip-point Bowies. There are T-handled versions; versions with small-radius concave blade edges called "gut hooks" designed to zip through skin or sever tendons while avoiding internal organs; versions with straight edges, and versions with edges so curved that they describe a quarter-circle. Each type has its champions and its detractors. The only criterion that really matters is what works for you, and the only way to find that out is to try different styles until you find one you're comfortable with.

RIVER, RESCUE, AND DIVING KNIVES

Rescue professionals, scuba divers, and whitewater paddlers demand a few common features of their knives. They often have to cut through rope or tough webbing material, and often have to do it quickly and in close proximity to human flesh. Consequently, knives for all three groups tend to feature serrated edges (good for cutting rope), and blunt tips (to avoid accidental stabbings). Folding rescue knives and sheaths for fixed-blade rescue knives usually have clips designed to keep them handy and secure outside of a pocket. The sheaths on some fixed-blade diving and river knives have a locking mechanism that holds the knife securely but allows it to be released quickly with one hand.

KNIVES YOU DON'T NEED

With so many worthwhile types of knives to consider carrying into the wilderness, it makes little sense to burden yourself with a knife of limited practicality. Some may find these knives enticing, but don't waste your time with…

THROWING KNIVES

Throwing knives have fixed, double-edge blades, and usually no handle grips—just a bare tang. They are made for one thing only: throwing. In the wilderness, the only plausible reason to throw a knife is to hunt game. And since hunting with a thrown knife is legal almost nowhere, the only reason to bring one (or more—they're often sold in sets of three) is because you expect to find yourself in a survival situation where you will be forced to hunt for your food. And if you expect to find yourself in this situation, and you still go, then there seems to be something seriously wrong with your thought processes. You'll never kill a rabbit with a thrown knife anyway, but you very well might lose it, which is probably the best thing to do with your silly throwing knife.

SWITCHBLADES, "AUTOMATICS," FLICK, AND GRAVITY KNIVES

These are all folding knives with quick-opening mechanisms. Switchblades and "automatics" are spring-loaded—you push a button or slide a thumb lever, and the blade pops out. Flick and gravity knives have a low-friction hinge and are configured so that, with a rapid wrist motion, the blade will swing out and usually lock with a lockback mechanism.

All four styles have been given the aura of menace through their appearance in movies and on television, but none are as durable and reliable as a well-made conventional folding knife. Their real purpose is to make the owner feel that he's a dangerous type, not to be messed with.

PRACTICAL ONE-HANDED OPENING

While it's doubtful that the quarter-second you might save with an "automatic" knife will ever confer a practical benefit, the ability to open a folding knife one-handed can be handy. The most practical one-handed folders are lockbacks with a tall blade whose spine sticks well out of the case when folded, and a thumb stud or hole near the top of the blade. By holding the case securely against the heel of your hand with four fingers, it's easy to lift the blade out by pushing with the thumb against the stud or hole.

BALISONGS

Also known as butterfly knives or fan knives, balisongs are folding knives popular in Indonesia and the Philippines. Having either single or double edges, they feature a two-part handle that hinges around the blade from opposite sides. It can be great fun to learn how to open and close a balisong one-handed, but the loose hinges that make one-handed opening possible also ensure that the blade will be wobbly and weak when deployed.

SURVIVAL KNIVES

There are survival knives and "survival knives." Almost any well-made knife—folding or fixed, plain-edge or serrated—can be credibly marketed as a survival knife, for almost any such knife will indeed help ensure your survival in the wilderness. But then there are faux survival knives that are designed mainly to look impressive in an action-movie-hero kind of way—knives with oversize (but often under-strength) blades, hollow (read "weak") handles containing miniature mockeries of survival kits, blade guards with toy "grappling hook" extensions, exaggerated and useless (but menacing-looking) teeth cut into the spine and, often, a tiny magnetic compass where the pommel should be, preventing the use of the butt as a hammer. They always have a feature called a blood groove, because that sounds really dangerous. Of course, the manufacturers of these "survival knives" don't put quotes around them, and they insist that theirs is the biggest, baddest, macho-est knife around. But you'll never see a skilled outdoorsperson carrying one of these ostentatious monstrosities.

DISPLAY AND NOVELTY KNIVES

Some knives are intended primarily as aesthetic objects, featuring elaborate blade shapes and handles decorated with precious metals and semi-precious stones, or laser-etched images commemorating some notable individual, event, or movie character. Some of these display knives consciously mimic the improbable edge weapons wielded by characters on the covers of fantasy novels. While such knives might be things of beauty or interest, they are not designed to give good service under rugged conditions. Leave them at home in a glass display case.

BOOT KNIVES

Boot knives are intended to be carried in a sheath inside the top of a tall boot, while neck knives are designed to be hung by a lanyard around the neck. Both types may be viable survival tools, but there's little reason to carry them in such awkward locations.

FINE POINTS

If all important knife characteristics were as visible as basic configuration (fixed versus folding), pattern and grind, and so on, then your choice of a knife would be as simple as looking at a photograph. But there are a few more important attributes to consider.

BALANCE AND FEEL

Perhaps a knife's most important quality is how it feels when you use it. This is mostly subjective, but if the knife doesn't feel right, then you may never feel quite safe using it, and it simply won't be very effective under those circumstances.

Consider the material, texture, and shape of the grip. A "tacky" rubber handle may help you keep your grip when your hands are wet or slippery. But you might find it uncomfortably sticky, and might prefer a hardwood handle with deep diamond-shaped cross-checking to ensure a solid grip. Some experts recommend that sheath knife handles have oval cross-sections, but a rectangular cross-section with rounded corners might fit your hand better. Unfortunately, just holding it in the store might not give you as good a sense for a knife's feel as spending an hour cutting tree limbs with it.

The knife's front-to-back balance influences both feel and function. A blade-heavy design, whose center of balance is forward of the handle, is better for chopping, while a light blade is easier to control for fine carving and whittling.

STEEL

It's rare that manufacturers describe the metallurgy of their blades in any detail—which is just as well, since it's a complex subject in which a lot of scientific jargon could easily be used to confuse the consumer. Most manufacturers do, though, identify a blade as either stainless or carbon (or high carbon) steel, and these are worth paying attention to.

A very small amount of carbon hardens steel. A certain amount of hardness is desirable, since hard steels hold an edge better. On the other hand, hard steels are harder to sharpen in the first place. Anything over 0.5% carbon is considered a "high carbon" steel. If you're willing to take out the stone on a moment's notice to touch up your knife, then a softer steel is for you. If you'd rather sharpen less often, you need a harder steel that holds the edge longer—but be prepared to spend more time creating that edge. The main drawback of carbon steel is its poor corrosion resistance.

Stainless steel contains at least 13% chromium, which improves the steel's resistance to both corrosion and wear. Most stainless steel is difficult to make and keep sharp, but some of the more expensive stainless steels avoid these drawbacks.

THE TANG

The tang is the part of the blade buried inside the handle of a fixed-blade knife.

A full tang is one that extends the whole length of the handle and from top to bottom—in other words, you can see the tang between the handle pieces all the way around.

Partial tangs come in three common varieties:

A half tang extends to the full height of the handle, but not to its whole length.

A push tang or stub tang extends only partway into the handle.

A rat-tail tang is like a push tang with a rod welded on the end that threads into a metal pommel at the butt.

A full tang is unquestionably the strongest design, and the best suited to being beaten on with a baton. But a full tang is also the heaviest design, and you may not like the feel of the steel against your hand. Half, push, and rat-tail tangs are lighter and provide cushioning all the way around.

QUALITY

Examine the knife carefully for signs of quality. Are all surfaces smooth and well-finished? Are the handle side-pieces secured firmly and the rivets fitted cleanly?

If it's a folding knife: do the hinges work smoothly? Is there any side-to-side play or wobble between the blade and the handle? Is the locking mechanism reliable, secure, and easy to operate?

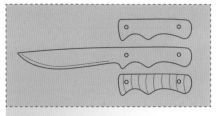

Full Tang

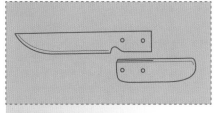

Half Tang

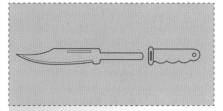

Push Tang

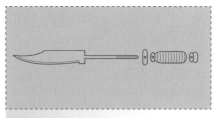

Rat-tail Tang

Avoid bells and whistles. At any given price, a knife with fewer "features" will probably have better materials and workmanship. Keep your ego in check. A bigger knife may not be what you need. Consider your likely requirements, and go for the best quality you're willing to afford.

		FULL TANG	PARTIAL TANG
Pro	✔	stronger	lighter
	✔	you can beat on the handle with a baton	less or no exposed metal—more comfortable
	✔	butt can be used as a hammer	
Cons	✘	heavier	handle likely to break if struck with a baton
	✘	exposed metal in the handle may feel uncomfortable	cannot use butt of handle as a hammer (except rat-tail)

MORS KOCHANSKI'S KNIFE ADVICE

Mors Kochanski is renowned as a survival expert, and his opinions are worthy of attention. In *Bushcraft: Outdoor Skills and Wilderness Survival*, he describes his sheath knife preferences:

- the blade should have a single edge
- the edge should be curved from the handle to the tip, with no straight section
- the blade should be carbon steel, ¹⁄₁₀" (2–2.5 mm) thick and 2" (20–25 mm) tall
- the back of the blade should be in line with the top of the handle
- the handle should be oval in cross-section
- there should be no upper blade guard
- the tang should be full
- there should be a strong pommel
- the knife should be strong enough to bear your weight if you drive it 4cm into a tree with the flat surface of the blade horizontal

CARRYING AND CARING FOR YOUR KNIFE

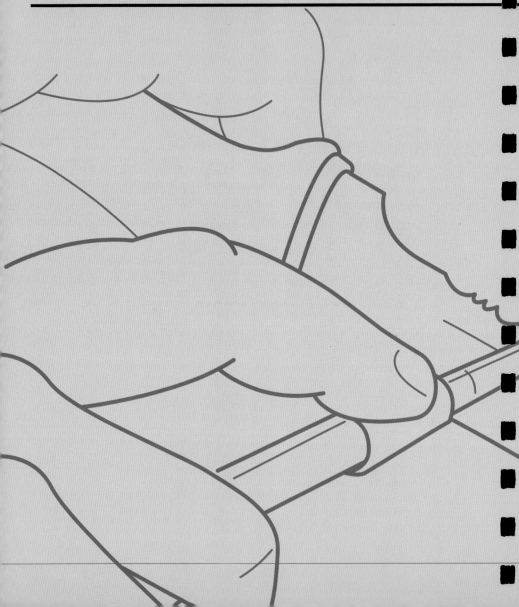

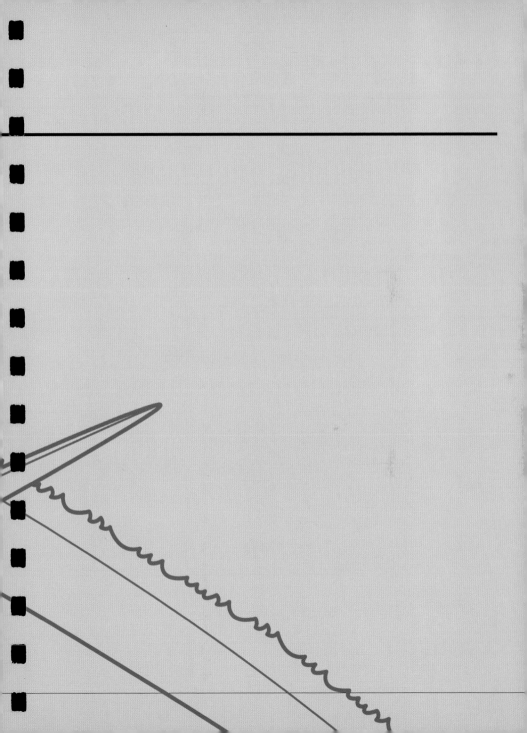

CARRY IT SAFELY

Unlike kitchen knives, most of which lead a sedentary life, outdoor knives are expected to move around. And while the blade of the stay-at-home kitchen knife is usually left exposed, the blade of an outdoor knife must be protected when being carried, for both the sake of its edge and of its owner's health. So fundamental is this consideration that the basic knife types are known by how they are carried: sheath knife, pocket knife, and belt folder.

BELT OR POCKET CLIPS

Some folding knives that are small enough to carry in your pocket are equipped with a clip, permitting them to be carried more conveniently within easy reach at the very top of a trouser pocket, or outside the pocket altogether. While fastening it to your belt is an obvious option, think about how you'll be dressed and equipped as you move through the wilderness, and consider clipping it instead to a piece of outerwear or equipment such as a shoulder strap or lashing point on your backpack, or a lash tab on a personal flotation device.

Don't place too much trust on the clip until you've tested it, because some clips are more

The clip on this lockback knife keeps it handy on your belt.

secure than others. Depending upon the clip, your knife might be bumped free from its attachment, and you may never notice that it's gone until too late.

WHERE'S YOUR SPARE?

If you enter the wilderness with more than one knife, make sure to keep them separately. If you lose one, you don't want to lose both. Even if you've got one on your belt and one in your pocket, consider packing at least one more.

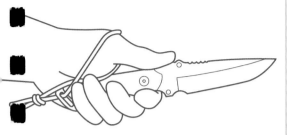

A well-designed sheath must protect the blade, hold the knife securely, and release it quickly and easily. A sheath that covers only the blade usually requires a snap-close strap near the top to secure the handle. If you find snapping and unsnapping the strap inconvenient, you might prefer a full-depth sheath that swallows almost the whole length of the knife, leaving only the pommel or lanyard exposed to grab hold of.

Leather is an excellent sheath material since it's easy on the blade, durable, and provides good protection, but it requires some care to prevent it from drying out and cracking. Ballistic nylon cloth requires no maintenance, but it's more prone to becoming cut up over time by the very blade it's meant to protect. Most hard plastic sheaths suffer neither of these drawbacks, although they are arguably the least attractive option.

LANYARDS

A lanyard hole is a feature found on many knives, and a good one to make use of. Thread any strong cord or a leather thong through the hole. If you make this just long enough to slip around your wrist, it will prevent you from dropping the knife on your foot or into the lake, should it slip from your hand. Or you might make the lanyard long enough so that it can remain tied to a belt loop while you use the knife.

SHEATHS

Almost all fixed-blade knives are sold with sheaths, for there is no safe way to carry them without one. When purchasing a new knife, consider the sheath as part of the purchase. A sheath of poor quality or design doesn't necessarily mean that the knife itself is of poor quality or design, but it will interfere with your use of the knife.

A good, simple leather sheath with a snap-close strap.

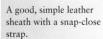

SHEATH LANYARD

Fixed-blade knives with long blades of 7" (18cm) or more can be awkward appendages when carried in a belt sheath—especially when you sit down and your thigh moves to a horizontal position while the sheath persists in remaining vertical. A lanyard or strap near the bottom of the sheath is meant to be fastened around your thigh, keeping the sheath and your thigh heading in the same direction. Not everyone finds it comfortable to walk with such an attachment, however.

TOOLS FOR SHARPENING KNIVES

Many knives need sharpening right out of the box, and all knives need to be sharpened regularly after every few hours of use. Many different tools for sharpening are available, and most will do a good job if used correctly. Choose the method that works best for you.

1 OIL STONES

Oil stones may be either natural stones or man-made from abrasives like aluminum oxide or silicon carbide. The natural versions—often known as Arkansas stones—tend to be more expensive. All types are available in various grits, with lower numbers being coarser and higher ones finer.

Coarse stones remove material more quickly, but leave a rougher edge. Unless a blade has been badly abused, you may not need a stone with a grit as coarse as 100. Most of your sharpening will be done with a medium-grit stone of 180–280, followed by a fine stone of 500–700. (These are U.S. standards. Comparable stones from Japanese manufacturers use a different measuring standard with consistently higher numbers.)

Oil stones use oil to lubricate the surface and suspend the microscopic metal-grinding debris so that the pores in the abrasive surface do not become clogged. Place several drops of light machine oil on an oil stone before use. When sharpening, pause occasionally to wipe it with a rag to remove the sludge, then apply a few more drops of oil.

2 WATER STONES

Water stones, which use water instead of oil as a lubricant, may also be either natural or synthetic. They must be soaked in water for several minutes before use. Less expensive than oil stones, they cut faster, but also wear faster and so need more maintenance.

Because of their lubricants, both water stones and oil stones can be somewhat messy to use.

1

2

This sort of hand-held sharpener, with carbide cutters at a pre-set angle, produces a quick but very poor, ragged edge. It is for people who don't want to learn how to sharpen a knife, and who can be content with one that doesn't perform well. Avoid.

Novices at knife sharpening often have trouble getting the right angle on the edge. Ceramic or diamond-coated crotch sticks pretty much ensure that you'll get the angle right as long as you keep the blade in a vertical plane. The downside is that you're limited to whatever angle is set by the tool itself.

3 CERAMIC STONES

Ceramic stones are more expensive and more durable than oil stones. They are used dry but must be cleaned frequently during use. Woodcarvers like ceramic stones because they can produce extremely sharp edges, but this may be overkill for an outdoors knife that will see rough use.

4 DIAMOND STONES

Diamond stones are actually steel plates with microscopic diamond crystals bonded to the surface. Unsurprisingly, they are the most expensive type of stone, and the most durable. A few drops of water on the surface will be enough to float the metal filings, making cleanup quick and easy. At any given grit, they cut faster than other stones.

3

4

SHARPENING METHODS

Read five articles on sharpening knives, and you'll likely learn five techniques. The method described here is one of many good approaches, and it's fairly easy to perform. Bear in mind that an outdoor knife does not need—and should not have—the ultimate in sharpness. The ruggedness of the edge is also an important quality.

SHARPENING IN STAGES

Depending upon the condition of the knife and how sharp you want to make it, the sharpening process may require two, three, four, or even five stages.

If the blade is very dull or nicked, start with a coarse stone. To restore a good edge after normal use, start with a medium stone, then proceed to a fine stone. If you want the finest edge possible, you may go one step further and strop the blade with a leather strap or synthetic strop (see page 41).

After a blade has been sharpened hundreds of times, it becomes shorter (measuring from the edge to the spine) and the edge becomes thicker, making it impossible to reestablish a narrow edge angle. When this occurs, you need to grind the sides flat to thin the blade before working on the edge angle.

LONG-TERM SHARPENING

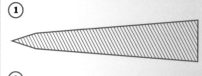

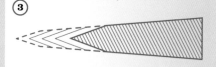

1. A new flat-ground blade, properly sharpened.

2. RIGHT: Before honing, grind the sides thinner to maintain the proper angle.

3. WRONG: After sharpening only the edge too many times, it becomes wider and the proper cutting angle cannot be maintained.

EDGE ANGLES

The smaller a blade's angle, the sharper it can be. Woodcarvers, who require precision above all, use a sharpening angle of just 8–10°. This promotes very accurate, clean cuts, but the edge is too fragile for outdoor use. It would be easily chipped, dulled, or "turned" if used for chopping or splitting wood, or making big, rough cuts. For our needs, a sharpening angle of 13–16° is more appropriate, producing an edge angle of 26–32°.

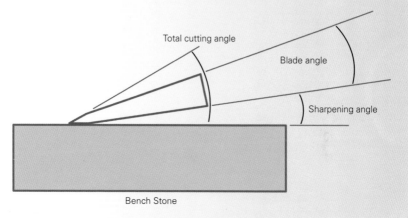

Total cutting angle

Blade angle

Sharpening angle

Bench Stone

A MATTER OF OPINION

There are different opinions regarding almost every step of the sharpening process, starting with the choice of tools. Some insist that only an oil stone (or a ceramic stone, or whatever) can do the best job. Some claim that the honing stroke must be toward the edge, and others claim just as adamantly that the edge must be trailed across the stone. Straight strokes versus circular motions; alternating sides on every stroke versus working one side completely before switching: if you listen to enough advice, you'll never get that knife sharp. Choose any method that appeals to you and learn to do it well. Then try another method if you wish and decide which one you prefer.

FLATTENING

There's almost no skill required to thin or flatten the blade—just persistence. Lay the blade flat against a coarse stone and stroke in a circular motion, gradually moving along the whole length of the blade to thin it consistently. Wipe or rinse off the grinding sludge periodically and reapply lubricant as required. After several dozen strokes, flip the knife over and do the other side. Then do the same with a medium stone, and finish with a fine stone to remove the scratches.

HONING

- Determine whether you need to begin with a coarse or medium stone. Hold the blade flat against the stone, then tip it on its edge so that the spine is about its own thickness above the stone. This will produce a sharpening angle between 13 and 16° on most blades. If you want to achieve a more precise result, use a protractor.

- Maintaining that angle, stroke the blade across the stone a dozen times or so, then flip it over and do the other side. If the edge is badly nicked or dented, you may need to do this several times, concentrating on the bad areas, then feathering these heavily ground areas in both directions to smooth out the line of the edge. You may stroke either toward or away from the edge, or back-and-forth. You may concentrate on one area of the blade before moving on to the next, or draw the blade

lengthwise across the stone as you stroke forward and back, so that the entire length of the blade gets equal treatment on every stroke. Pressure should be moderate—just enough so that you can feel the stone abrading the steel.

- When you're done with the coarse or medium stone, move on to the fine stone and repeat the process. Just five or ten strokes may suffice for each side.

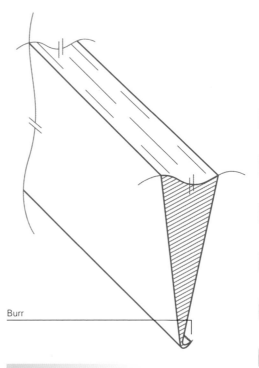

Burr

It is essential to remove the burr after honing. Failure to do so will cause it to break off during use, leaving a poor edge.

TESTING FOR SHARPNESS

How do you know when the blade is sharp enough? There are several tests:

- Take a thin shaving across the end grain of a pine board. The cut should be smooth, with no torn fibers.
- Try slicing a piece of expanded polystyrene (e.g., Styrofoam). Do the cells slice cleanly, or do they compress and bunch up?
- Can you slice through the edge of a piece of writing paper?
- A method not to use: shaving your arm or your neck.

A good bench-quality sharpening stone is too big and heavy to carry into the field, but pocket-size stones are available. An excellent option for portability is the kind of diamond sharpener shaped like a file.

What if you're in the wilderness with no sharpening equipment? Well, you never are! Almost any stone with a fairly regular surface can be used to sharpen a knife. With just a little searching, you may be able to find 100 percent natural stones in coarse, medium, and fine.

It is safer to draw the knife across a hand-held stone than vice versa. Even so, make sure you hold the stone so as not to endanger your fingers, and stroke away from your torso and other arm.

STROPPING

- Check the edge by dragging your thumb across it from the spine toward the edge. Caution: do NOT run your thumb along the edge! Your use of the fine stone may have left the edge perfectly clean. But if you feel a burr, this must be removed, either by further honing on the fine stone, or by stropping.

- You may use a leather strap, an old belt, or a piece of tough cotton fabric fastened securely to a thin board. Charge the strop with stropping powder or household abrasive cleanser. Drag the blade across the strop a dozen times on each side, trailing the edge. Check for the burr and repeat as needed.

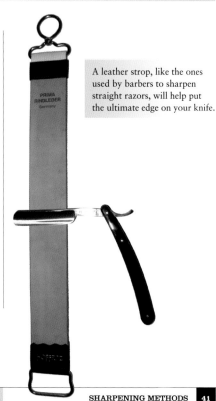

A leather strop, like the ones used by barbers to sharpen straight razors, will help put the ultimate edge on your knife.

SHARPENING SERRATED BLADES

Serrations increase the effective length of a blade, so that a 3" (8cm) blade may have 4–5" (10–13cm) of cutting edge. Because of this, serrated blades retain their sharpness longer than plain blades of comparable length. That's a good thing, since they're more difficult to sharpen.

SERRATION SHAPE

Serrations are generally ground on only one side of the blade and are often of different sizes and shapes. An edge may have two or three small-radius serrations between every large-radius one, and the bevel angles of the different-size serrations may differ as well. All of this has implications for sharpening techniques.

SHARPENING TOOLS

The best tool for sharpening a serrated knife is a set of round, tapered sharpening rods. Available in a variety of grits, these are made from abrasive ceramic, or steel with minute diamond grains embedded in the surface. Because of their conical shape, they can be used for serrations of different radii.

If your knife has a single serration size, a cylindrical rod makes sense, because you can use the entire length of the tool without fear of altering the size of the serration. Make sure to get the right size tool by bringing your knife into the store and comparing the tool's diameter against the serrations.

SETUP

If you're right-handed, and the serrations are ground on the left side of the blade, hold the sharpener in your right hand and the knife in your left. Although this can be done freehand, it's easier and more accurate to rest the knife on a workbench or other solid object, with the edge facing away from you, and the blade tilted so that the bevel of the serrations is horizontal.

If you're left-handed, or if the serrations are ground on the right side of the blade, you might find it easier to make the tool the stationary object, and use your dominant hand to stroke the knife against it. In that case, place the handle end of the sharpening tool on the bench, and rest the opposite end against your chest, holding it steady with your off hand.

TIP

Remember that although a dull serrated knife may make its way through material more easily than a dull plain edge, it will do so by tearing rather than slicing, leaving a ragged cut.

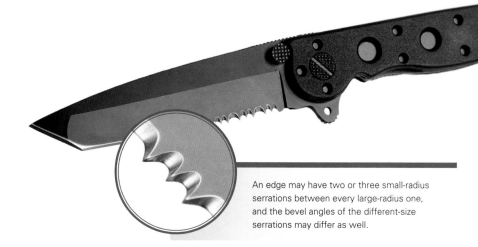

An edge may have two or three small-radius serrations between every large-radius one, and the bevel angles of the different-size serrations may differ as well.

TECHNIQUE

Some people can stroke the tool against the blade in both directions while keeping the angles steady. If you find this difficult, make your strokes all in one direction, from the back of the blade toward the edge. This causes the burr to form on the non-serrated side of the blade, where it is easier to remove. It also keeps the edge facing away from the off hand, so that an errant stroke doesn't result in a laceration. If you do stroke in both directions, be extra careful of the edge.

ALTERNATE TECHNIQUES

Here are some more tips for sharpening a serrated knife:

- Set up a 2x4 or other piece of lumber as a solid workbench. You want something narrow enough to reach across easily. Use clamps to hold the blade flat against the wood, with the serrated side up and the edge facing away from you and hanging over the edge. This enables you to use both hands to control the sharpening tool. Relocate the clamps when necessary.

- Instead of an expensive diamond-encrusted sharpening tool, cut a sheet of 300- or 600-grit wet-or-dry sandpaper into narrow strips and wrap them around a short section of dowel or metal rod that matches the diameter of the serration. A bicycle spoke is about right for some small-radius serrations.

- With a black felt-tip pen, completely ink over the bevels on all the serrations before you begin sharpening. It will take just a stroke or two with the sharpening tool to see whether you're working at the right angle. Use the trick only with wet-dry sandpaper: you don't want to transfer ink to ceramic or diamond/steel tools.

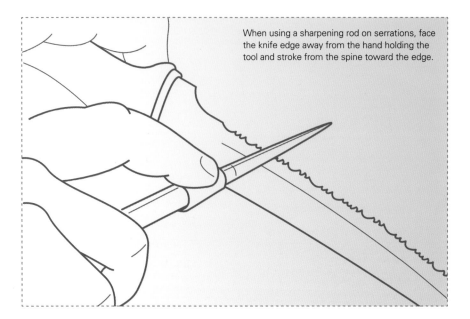

When using a sharpening rod on serrations, face the knife edge away from the hand holding the tool and stroke from the spine toward the edge.

- For general sharpening, start with a medium- or fine-grit rod. In cases of deferred maintenance, you may need to start with the coarse one. Find the section along the length of the rod that fits snugly into the serration, and take gentle strokes. Keep the strokes short so that you don't change the radius of the serration.

- After a stroke or two, look carefully at the serration. A consistent pattern of scratches will indicate that you're maintaining the existing bevel angle. If the serration is scratched only at the top or bottom, adjust your angle of attack.

- After five or ten strokes, feel the back of the blade to check whether a burr has developed. If not, take five or ten more strokes and check again.

- Once a burr has formed, move along to the next serration. If the blade has serrations of different sizes, do all the serrations of one size before moving on to the other size or sizes.

- After you've done all the serrations, flip the knife over and remove the burrs. On anything but a hollow-ground blade, you can use either the same sharpening rod, or a fine stone, or a strop. On a hollow-ground blade, you must use a strop, because a stone will remove the tips of the teeth. Finish up by stropping alternately on both sides, trailing the edge as you drag the blade across the leather.

MAKE IT HANDIER

As well-designed as many knives are, many can still be improved with some simple modifications. If you experiment, make sure to test your modifications thoroughly before heading into the wilderness, where your safety may depend upon them.

IMPROVE THE GRIP

No part of a knife is more subjective than the grip. Objectively, it just needs not to fall apart. But what's comfortable and what feels secure are matters of opinion, so feel free to make some changes.

After scoring the handle with a fine-tooth saw, use a triangular file to shape the grooves for a better grip.

A smooth wood or hard plastic grip can be modified with carefully incised scoring to improve your hold on it. Unless you're an expert carver, this is best done with a fine, sharp file. In the case of a wood grip, you'll want to treat the handle with oil or varnish again to protect the wood after you've scored it. Warning: some plastic grips may crumble or chip if you score their surface deeply.

On a sheath knife, a "grippier" grip can also be achieved by applying a non-slip material to the handle. A section of inner tube from a low-profile bicycle tire can be slipped over the handle, and may be secure without any adhesive. Of course, this will increase the thickness of the handle, which may or may not be desirable.

Another way to make the handle thicker is to wrap it with duct tape. While some will hate the way this feels or looks, others won't mind, and you will always have a few feet of this invaluable survival material ready to hand.

ADD A LANYARD HOLE

A lanyard helps protect your knife from loss, and a wrist lanyard can help increase the speed of the knife blade when making swinging strokes, for more effective wood chopping. (See page 62.) If your knife has no lanyard hole, add one if possible.

First determine if the pommel can be drilled. This is rarely a problem on a sheath knife with a full tang or a push tang, unless a rivet

ANGLING THE SHEATH

If you find that the sheath of your long knife gets in the way and you don't want to use a sheath lanyard (see page 35), you can modify the belt loop as shown, resewing or gluing material so that the knife hangs at a forward-facing angle.

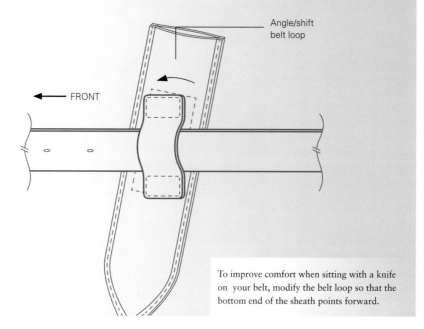

Angle/shift belt loop

← FRONT

To improve comfort when sitting with a knife on your belt, modify the belt loop so that the bottom end of the sheath points forward.

is in the way. A rat-tail tang, however, may have a threaded rod right where you'd like to place the lanyard hole, and you should not attempt to drill through this or the knife will fall apart. Many folding knives cannot be drilled without compromising their structure or function.

Don't attempt to freehand the hole. Drilling requires a drill press with a high-speed bit and a drill press vice to hold the knife. After drilling, chamfer the hole on both sides.

IMPROVE THE SHEATH

The sheath can be a handy and logical place to attach a sharpening stone. How you go about it will depend upon the material of the sheath. A small pocket, just large enough to hold a miniature stone, can be sewn onto the front of a fabric or leather sheath. With a hard plastic sheath, fastening the stone with epoxy is often a better approach, although epoxy may not stick to all types of plastic.

IMPROVISE A KNIFE

Throughout this book, we assume that even if you lose all your other gear, you've still got your knife, and that will see you through almost any difficulties. But what if you lose your knife? All may not be lost if you can improvise one from materials in your environment.

A KNIFE, OR A BLADE?

First, get rid of your preconception of what a knife should look like, and concentrate on essentials. Your "knife" might not require a handle, and the blade need not necessarily be long and thin. If the job at hand requires puncturing rather than slicing, it might not even require an edge: a simple point might suffice.

FLINT KNAPPING

Many stones can be crafted into usable knife blades, but hard, fine-grained stones like flint, chert, and obsidian can be crafted into fine thin blades with extremely sharp edges.

If the stone you've chosen is large, use another stone that fits comfortably in your hand to use as a hammer, and strike the workpiece on its "end grain" to break

Primitive knives don't need handles to be effective. A sharp-edged piece of flint can perform many cutting tasks.

OTHER MATERIALS

Several materials can be used to make improvised knives. Other than bamboo, few woods can be sharpened to take an edge sufficient for slicing, but almost any wood or a piece of antler can be sharpened to a point for puncturing tasks. (See page 75 for advice on fire-hardening wood.)

Almost any scrap of metal can be sharpened against a stone, and a handle improvised only if desired. Even broken glass can serve as a useful blade, although a handle is a near necessity to avoid cutting your hand.

off large flakes. If your workpiece is small enough to hold in one or both hands, find another rock to use as a stationary anvil, and strike the workpiece against it. This is a crude process, and you will probably have to break off dozens of pieces before you get one that suits your needs.

FLINT KNAPPING

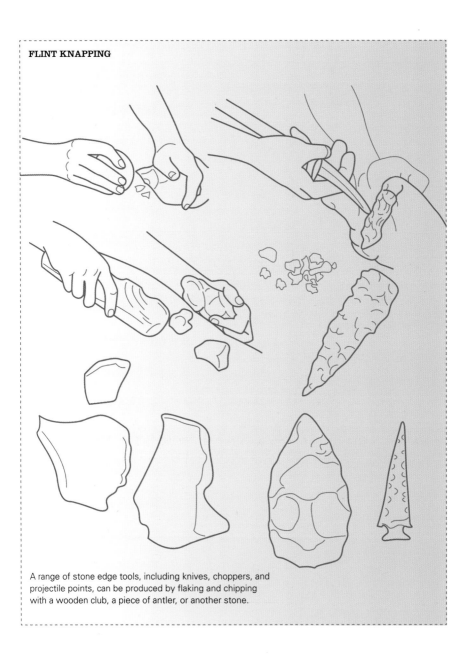

A range of stone edge tools, including knives, choppers, and projectile points, can be produced by flaking and chipping with a wooden club, a piece of antler, or another stone.

Holding your workpiece in one hand, strike the edge carefully with a small hammer stone to refine the edge. If you will use the stone as a knife without a handle, you might also work on the back edge to remove any sharp edges that will interfere with your grip. To make the most refined edge, carefully remove small flakes from the edge by "pressure flaking" rather than striking it, using a blunt-pointed piece of hardwood or antler as a tool.

HAFTING THE KNIFE

If your stone blade is long enough to have a tang, a handle can be added. A small stick, split in half, will make a nicely rounded handle. This can be lashed in place with rawhide, string, wire, or strips of bark. For that matter, the stick may not be needed if sufficient wraps of binding material are placed around the tang.

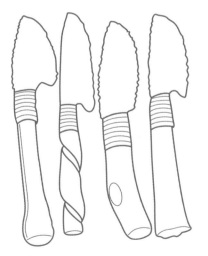

Hafted stone knives.

MAKE A HOKO KNIFE

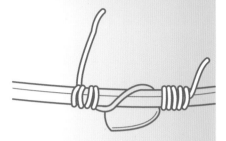

At an archaeological site on the Hoko River on the Strait of Juan de Fuca in Washington state, in a village that had been covered by a mudslide some 2,500 years ago, archaeologists found elegant little slicing knives that are easy to reproduce. Only a small stone flake is required, but it must be thin and very sharp. A green stick 7–9" (18–23cm) long serves as the handle. Willow works well for both the handle and the binding material.

Strip bark from the stick in long thin strips. Tie a strip around the stick about 4" (10cm) from one end, then split the stick lengthwise, using a sharp sliver of stone as a temporary blade. The bark tie will prevent the split from running too far. Next, push your designated blade flake into the slot at least 1" (2.5cm) beyond the end of the handle and remove the bark tie. Place one end of the binding strip in the slot on the "tip" end of the knife, take a turn around the stick, and tie a simple overhand knot around the stick and against the flake. Take another turn or two, then angle the bark toward the back of the handle. Make another turn or two against the other end of the flake, finishing with an overhand knot.

This is an excellent knife for fine slicing tasks and cleaning fish.

USING A KNIFE

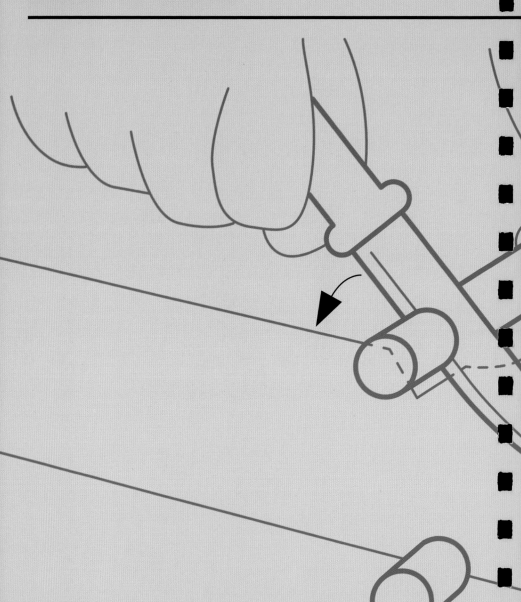

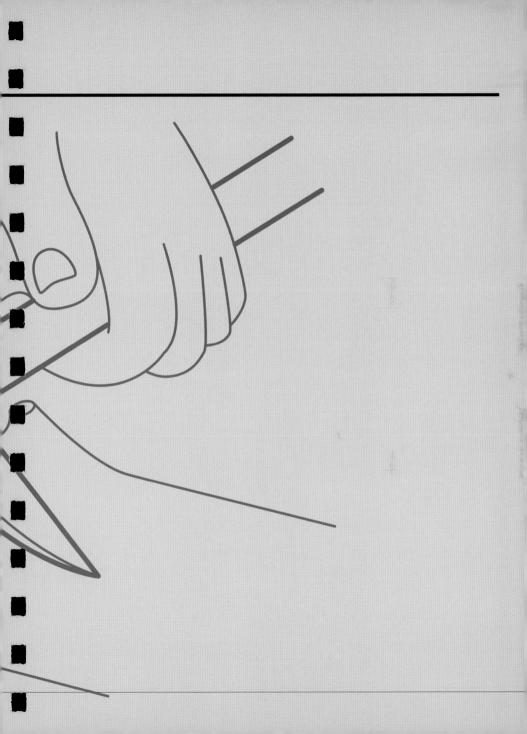

KEEP IT SAFE AND LEGAL

Knives cut. Forgive the obvious but, even while understanding that risk, people continually cut themselves with knives. The point isn't that knives are dangerous—we all know that. The point is that there are ways to use knives that significantly reduce the risk of accidents.

RISKS

A key aspect of knife safety is understanding the specific risks—the circumstances in which a knife is likely to slip, leading to a loss of control and a possible encounter with an inconveniently placed body part.

SAFE GRIP

Different cutting tasks may force the handle in different directions, requiring a different grip on the handle. Likewise, the workpiece must be held, positioned, or secured in such a way that errant knife strokes will not cause injury. Both of these issues are addressed in the following chapters.

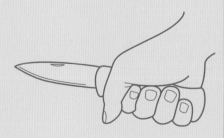

SAFE SURROUNDINGS

Errant knife strokes can also injure other people nearby, and the knife user must make sure that people remain a safe distance away. This is especially true of children, who may need to be reminded often to keep their distance.

SAFE KNIFE

A knife that breaks during use will almost certainly go out of control and will probably cause injury. That's why it's important to use the right knife for the job, and avoid subjecting a knife to stresses beyond its designed use. A thin blade is likely to shatter if used to pry, and when breaking it could either slip in a dangerous direction, or shoot a chip of metal into your eye. Even thicker blades can snap or shatter if abused, although softer steel is more likely to bend than break.

Sharp knives are safer than dull ones. That may seem counterintuitive until you understand that a sharp knife cuts more easily, requiring less force to do the job. Should the knife slip, or should the workpiece pare more readily than expected, it's much easier to control the knife if you were pushing it gently than if you were bearing down hard.

Folding knives should generally be confined to straightforward cutting tasks. Any prying, twisting, or pounding procedure that severely strains the hinge might result in breakage or, at the very least, in weakening the hinge, reducing the knife's effectiveness and safety, and making future breakage more likely.

Higher-quality knives are less likely to break, but all are subject to wear. Examine your knives carefully, and repair or replace any that show signs of weakness.

KNIVES AND THE LAW

Knife laws can vary from state to state or province to province within a single country, and of course different countries maintain their own criminal laws. In some U.S. states, for example, carrying a knife with a blade more than 3" (8cm) long in your pocket might contravene concealed weapons laws, while other states have no such concerns. Some jurisdictions consider a big sheath knife just another practical edge tool, while others classify it as a dangerous weapon. Check with local law-enforcement authorities to find out what you can legally carry and whether it may be concealed upon your person.

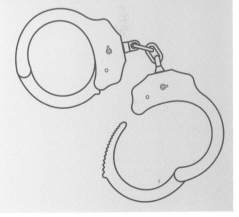

CHILDREN AND KNIVES

One hundred and fifty years ago, it was common for a rural American schoolboy to carry a knife everywhere. Boys would play mumbledy-peg in schoolyards and whittle for diversion. Today, carrying a knife to school would result in immediate expulsion and maybe a trip to the police station. But children today are not more dangerous or less responsible than their great-great-grandparents, and there's no reason why a responsible child can't have and use a knife—after receiving proper guidance.

According to the American Knife & Tool Institute, teaching knife safety requires "the three Rs... repetition, reinforcement, and role models," along with a fourth, "respect." Every parent must decide when a child is ready to handle a knife. When that time comes, it is essential to teach the rules of knife safety and to be prepared to enforce them by confiscation if violated.

Parents of children who are too young to handle a knife safely should do what is necessary to keep their children safe, while parents of children who are old enough should encourage their responsible use of a practical tool.

SAFE USE

Many common knife tasks are associated with particular accidents. Splitting firewood, for example, poses different risks than cutting a tree limb. See the following chapters for specific safety measures for specific tasks.

No matter how robust a lockback mechanism, never use a folding knife in such a way that the blade might close on your fingers or hand. With the exception of throwing knives, which have no place in your outdoor emergency kit (see page 26), knives are not meant to be thrown. Avoid horseplay and refuse to participate in any knife "game" that involves an intentional threat to life or limb.

HOLDING THE KNIFE

A proper grip on the knife maximizes control for making accurate cuts and avoiding injury. Most knife injuries are the result of inattention or a sudden loss of control. In most cases of inattention, the injury is to the fingers or hand holding or steadying the workpiece: it's uncanny how you can place your own finger beneath the knife blade and then proceed to cut! Loss-of-control injuries can be worse—even life-threatening—because the knife might penetrate vital organs or major blood vessels.

THE BASIC GRIP

Most cuts are made with a grip so simple that there is no formal word for it: we'll call it the basic grip. The fingers wrap around the handle, and are joined on the same side by the thumb, the side of which presses against the handle. This is a strong grip, good for the heaviest cutting tasks.

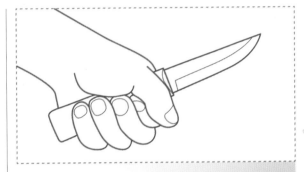

Basic grip.

You can get better control by moving your thumb to the top of the handle, and moving your other fingers slightly more toward the bottom. By moving the thumb forward, so that it is over the spine and just in front of the handle, even more control is gained, but at the expense of power.

Modified basic grip with thumb over the spine.

GRIPS FOR CAREFUL WORK

For very delicate work, rotate the knife 180° around its axis and move your whole hand forward so that only your third, fourth, and fifth fingers remain on the handle. Your index finger is curved loosely over the spine, and your thumb steadies the blade on the other side. This grip is possible only on a knife with no upper guard.

When holding the knife this way, the edge naturally faces your torso. This grip should not be used for cutting down or away from yourself. Do not use this grip for heavy work, as there is a real risk of cutting your fingers.

HOLDING A SHEEPSFOOT BLADE

With a sheepsfoot blade (see page 19), the hand can be moved all the way over the blade, which is held firmly between the thumb on one side, and the index and middle fingers on the other. This provides the ultimate in control for very light-duty operations, but it is dangerous for any other. In fact, this blade pattern was invented to give shepherds good control when trimming sheeps' hooves.

The "careful work grip" gives good control, but must be used with caution.

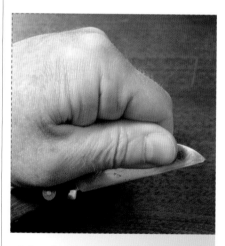

A sheepsfoot blade can be held entirely on the steel for careful scraping or extremely close work with the point.

HOLDING THE WORKPIECE

For many knife tasks, the workpiece must be held or steadied by the "off" hand, and sometimes other body parts come into play as well. This inevitably poses a risk of injury, unless care is taken in how the part is held. By safely securing the workpiece, the work can be done more precisely and quickly.

THE RULE OF THUMB ... AND FINGERS AND ALL THE REST

Any time you're about to begin cutting, look at yourself. Examine your position and think about the direction of the knife. Are any body parts in the way? How about if the knife slips? In what direction would your hand and knife travel if the wood were to separate unexpectedly, or if you were to hit an unexpected knot that might deflect your stroke? Would the knife then head toward your body?

It's surprisingly common for people to slice their own thumb when stripping bark from a stick, simply because they place their thumb right in the path of the knife. The solution, of course, is to hold the stick above where the cut will begin, but the real problem isn't one of technique: it's one of not paying attention.

SAFE WORKHOLDING

It is often convenient to brace a workpiece against your thigh or chest while holding it with your off hand. This is fine as long as you follow certain safety rules.

When working in a sitting position, rest your elbows on your knees and hold the workpiece in front of them, so that your knife strokes away from your thighs. For a longer workpiece, another approach is to place it crosswise over your thighs, starting the cut to the outside of your on-side leg, and stroke away from your body. In other words, a right-handed carver with a stick across his thighs will stroke only to the right of his right thigh.

When making strong cuts that involve a follow-through, make sure the direction is away from your trunk and limbs.

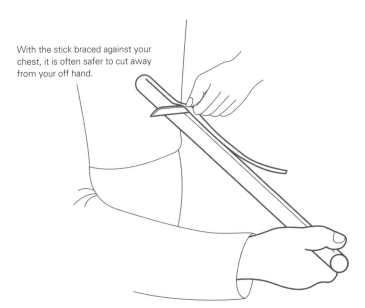

With the stick braced against your chest, it is often safer to cut away from your off hand.

BRACING A WORKPIECE AGAINST YOUR CHEST

When bracing a workpiece against your chest, it may be difficult to position your off hand in such a way as to avoid danger on a downward stroke. It is often safer to cut toward your torso. This requires a different grip. Turn the knife over so that your knuckles are along the top of the handle and the blade faces toward you. Rest the side of your thumb on the upper side of the blade, and lock your wrist so that the knife edge is parallel to your chest or even pointing a little away from it. Draw the knife slowly upward along the top of the workpiece. Should the knife slip, your elbow's limited range of motion will prevent the knife from reaching your chest. Take care that the workpiece is held low on your chest, and that the knife's direction can not lead it up to your face in case of a slip. Hold the elbow of your off hand high and away from your torso to keep it out of the way of an errant stroke.

When cutting through or pointing a stick, it is often convenient to use the thumb of your knife hand to press the workpiece against the blade. To avoid a cut when the knife breaks through, make sure to hold your thumb off to the side, not directly in the blade's path. Likewise, whenever you use the thumb of your knife hand to stabilize the workpiece, keep it clear of the direction of cut.

Don't cradle a small workpiece in the palm of your hand. Instead, support it on a solid surface, such as a log, and hold it by the edges. If cutting into the end of a small stick, don't hold the workpiece close beneath the blade. Hold it lower down or, better yet, place the stick flat on a solid surface and cut it from the side.

When pushing down with a folding knife, keep your fingers away from the blade slot by holding the knife only along the top of the handle. No matter how robust a lockback mechanism may appear, do not trust it to prevent the blade from folding up on your fingers when working the knife hard.

With a long stick resting across both thighs, stroke toward the "on" side.

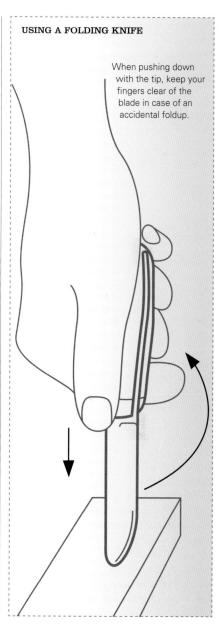

USING A FOLDING KNIFE

When pushing down with the tip, keep your fingers clear of the blade in case of an accidental foldup.

BASIC CUTTING TECHNIQUES

With these basic techniques and a sharp knife of good quality, you can do an astonishing amount of work quickly. Learn and practice these skills before you need them in a survival situation, and you'll come to rely on your knife as a tool with almost unlimited utility.

HIP CUT

This is a good method for cutting a stick to length, or carving a blunt point. Because this powerful cut can take off a big chunk of wood in a single stroke, it involves a big follow-through. Make sure the area behind and to your on side is clear of people and obstructions.

Setup

Hold the stick in your off hand, with your thumb toward the end to be cut. Cross the arm over your belly and rest your wrist against your on-side hip so that the working end of the stick points down and behind you. Hold the knife in a basic grip.

Cutting Action

Raise your onside shoulder and bend the elbow. Push down vigorously on the knife, mainly using power from your shoulder. Toward the end of the cut, your elbow will straighten and your lower arm will swing behind you and toward your on side.

CROSS-CHEST CUT

This method is suitable for pieces too short for the hip cut. As described, it's a rough, powerful cut, but it is also useful for thinning a stick and trimming knots if performed with more finesse. The follow-through is in front of you, up and toward the on side.

When using the hip cut, the follow-through will be down and to the "on" side.

Setup

Hold the knife in a reverse grip, with the fingers wrapped around the top of the handle and the cutting edge facing toward you. Hold the workpiece fairly close to the working end, but make sure your fingers are not in the way of the cut. Your hands will nearly meet in the middle of your chest, with the blade pointing up and the edge toward your on side.

The follow-through of the powerful cross-chest cut is up and away from the on-side shoulder.

Cutting Action

Use your back muscles to draw your knife hand and off hand apart simultaneously, so that your elbows move out to the sides. Both the knife and the workpiece will move against each other.

THUMB-ASSISTED CUT

This is a good way to cut a deep single notch in a short stick, or to notch a stick all the way around. It uses a similar body position as the cross-chest cut, but a different grip on the knife. There is no follow-through. It can only be used with a knife that has no upper blade guard.

Setup

Hold the knife with the top of the handle facing your wrist, the second row of knuckles at the bottom of the handle, and your thumb against the spine of the blade just beyond the hilt. Both arms will be held in front of your chest at about 45° from vertical.

Cutting Action

Holding the blade across the stick, make the "stop cut" by pressing the blade in perpendicular to the surface, using power from your thumb to supplement the power from your wrist. Make a second cut about 1" (2.5cm) below the stop cut at a 45° angle, so that it meets the bottom of the stop cut. Repeat if you wish to notch the stick all the way around.

LANYARD CHOPPING

Most knives lack the heft to chop wood unassisted, so cutting, rather than chopping, using the methods above, is generally a more effective way of turning a long stick into sections.

Long, heavy sheath knives can, however, do an adequate job chopping sticks up to about 3" (8cm) diameter. This can be aided with an especially sturdy lanyard, which enables you to hold the knife securely at the very end of the handle. By extending the knife just 1–2" (2.5–5cm) farther, you increase the speed of its swing and thus increase its momentum, resulting in a deeper cut. Chopping, of course, is done by making an ever-deepening V-shaped notch. Turning the stick allows you to limit the depth of the notch to a maximum of the stick's radius.

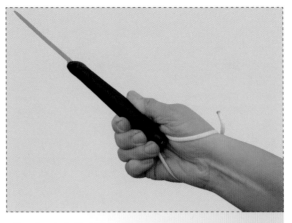

To swing the knife while holding it at the very end of the handle, the lanyard must be exactly the right length and very secure.

In addition to being strong, the lanyard must be just the right length to lie firmly against your wrist while keeping the end of the handle solidly in your hand. If the lanyard is too long, you risk losing control of the knife.

Press the blade into the workpiece with the thumb-assisted cut.

BATON CHOPPING

With the use of a baton—which is simply a stick of the right length and heft—even smaller sheath knives become effective chopping tools. Almost any hardwood stick 10–12" (25–30cm) long and 1–2"(2.5–5cm) in diameter will do a good job. Don't use a stone. It could damage your knife or send chips into your eyes.

Place the blade against the work, with the tip extending beyond it. Use the baton to hammer against the spine directly over the work. Push down on the handle at the moment of impact to keep the blade straight and provide extra force

CUTTING THROUGH A STICK

Cuts are made in pairs, forming a V-shaped notch. Make the first cut at about 30° from the vertical, then the next at the same angle but from the opposite direction, so that the notch has an angle of about 60°. Turn the stick and repeat, with the second notch joining the first. Continue turning the stick until you've worked all the way through. For a thicker stick, you may need to go all the way around more than once.

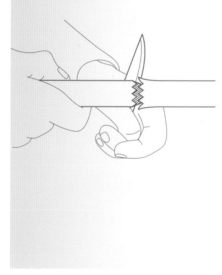

BATON SPLITTING

Splitting wood with a baton is similar to chopping. Don't try to split pieces that are too large. Your blade must be at least a couple inches (5cm) longer than diameter of the wood.

Hold the stick vertical, preferably on a stump or a downed log. Press your blade into the end-grain at the top, with at least 2" (5cm) of blade extending beyond the work. Holding the stick vertical with the knife, strike the spine of the blade, pressing down with your off hand on the handle.

When the split is nearly complete, you can twist the knife to complete the split.

Batoning—striking the spine of the knife with a wooden club—is an effective way to chop wood.

behind the blow. For small limbs, a straight cut may suffice, but heavier work requires a V-shaped notch consisting of two cuts at opposing angles. If the cut is so deep that you can no longer hit the spine directly over the work, hit it on the tip of the knife as close to the work as possible.

TREE WORK

The days are long gone when outdoorspeople would cut fresh fir boughs to make a comfortable bed for the night. Trees are too valuable a resource to treat with such profligacy, and even relatively inexperienced campers now know not to cut live ones. Of course, it's also illegal on most public lands and all private land without the owner's permission. That said, we're talking about survival. No-one will object to you cutting down a live tree if your life depends upon it.

LIMBING A STANDING TREE

If a tree's trunk is small enough to reach around and see around, the best way to cut off small, low limbs is from the opposite side, using a baton. The trunk protects you from the knife's follow-through when the final stroke breaks through the limb. When cutting larger limbs in this manner, a helper can bend the bough down, stressing the wood fibers. They will cut much more readily this way, and maintaining downward pressure on the limb keeps the cut open so that the knife does not bind. Cut where the bend is at its maximum, and make sure the helper is clear of the baton and the knife's follow-through. Also be aware that a stressed limb or trunk can spring back dangerously when the pressure is released on cut-through.

If the trunk is too large to work from the opposite side, work with your arms extended and stand well clear when breakthrough is imminent. Use a V-notch cut if the limb is too thick for a straight-through approach.

It is often safer and more convenient to work around the trunk when baton-chopping a limb.

FELLING

If you're able to bend a tree trunk, you should be able to fell it with a fixed-blade knife and a baton. This generally means a maximum diameter of about 3" (8cm), although this varies considerably with the particular tree and the length of your knife blade.

Bend the trunk down as far as you can. Trees that don't bend readily with a single effort can often be loosened by repeated bending so that eventually you can hold it down with your off hand. If you are working alone, batoning is not an option. Slice into the trunk at a steep angle while the fibers are being stretched, and rock the blade forward and back. You may be surprised how effective this is. Since you'll be working with your face close to the cut, be especially wary of spring-back when the cut nears completion.

A helper can make things much easier, holding down a larger trunk with his whole weight than you can with just your off hand. By freeing your off hand, the helper makes possible the use of the baton.

Use the same principles of bending, stressing and slicing when working on the limbs or the top of a down tree. You may find it convenient to bend the limb to the ground and hold it there with your foot, but make sure your on-side leg is clear of your follow-through.

It's surprisingly easy to slice through a sapling with a knife if you bend the trunk down to stress and expose the wood fibers.

NOTCHES AND HOLES

The techniques described in the previous chapter are suitable for completing fairly large-scale projects: building shelter, getting firewood, and such. Small-scale projects such as toolmaking require more refined skills—less muscle and more finesse.

END NOTCHING

Being able to produce a square-bottom notch, or nock, in the end of a stick is a valuable toolmaking skill, useful for both ends of arrows and hafting stone knives and axe heads. A stick with nocks at both ends makes a handy reel for fishing line.

The process will shorten the stock by at least 1" (2.5cm), so start with a stick an inch or two longer than the finished piece will be. Begin by making a small V-notch on the stick where you want the bottom of the nock. The length of the V-notch should be the same as the width of the nock. Turn the stick over and make another V-notch on the opposite side.

Turn the stick 90° and make another V-notch where the end of the stick will be cut off, then flip it over and cut another V-notch opposite it.

Place your blade in one of the V-notches nearer the end and, as you cut in, angle it parallel to the surface of the stick. Draw it down until it reaches the lower V-notches. Do the same on the other side. Use the tip of your knife to dig straight into the lower V-notches and break loose the end scrap.

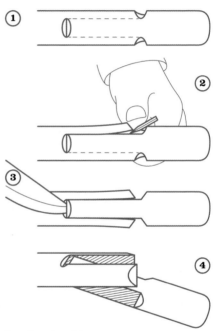

To end-notch a stick:

1. Start with two pairs of V-notches oriented 90° from each other and spaced about 1" (2.5cm) apart.
2. Cut from the upper notches down to the outside edges of the lower notches.
3. Use the tip of the knife to deepen the cuts at the lower notches.
4. Remove the scrap.

SHEARING

A small stick can be quickly cut into multiple sections by turning a fixed-blade knife into a shear. On a solid, down log, excavate a narrow hollow just beneath a knot, so that you can insert several inches of blade at an angle of roughly 45°. Place the workpiece under the blade and press down on the handle. The knot should keep the tip in place and act as a fulcrum, allowing you to apply a great deal of pressure.

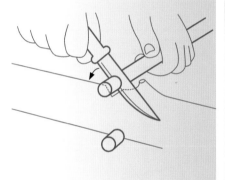

By cutting the lower V-notches first, you avoid splitting the stick farther than the desired bottom of the nock.

HOLE CARVING

A small square hole can be carved through a stick with a fine-pointed knife. A clip-point blade is a good tool for this job. The thickness of the stick and the width of your knife's tip will determine how small you can make the hole, but there is essentially no maximum size.

It's much easier to carve a hole through a stick if you thin it from both sides first.

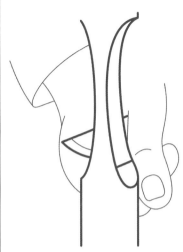

Begin with deep V-notches on both sides, then make a series of oblique slicing cuts down to the notch, removing each long, thin "chip" as you go. Work equally from both sides of the stick until it is thin enough.

Push the tip of the knife straight down across the grain of the wood, until it cuts to the width of the desired hole. Depending on the sizes of the knife and the hole desired, you might need to turn the knife around and cut the width in two steps, with the edge facing left and then right. If the first cut was the top edge of the hole, repeat the process to define the bottom edge. Next, push the tip of the knife between the top and bottom cuts along the grain and pry out some wood. Do the same to create the right and left edges of the hole, then turn the stick over and repeat these steps.

FOOD WITH A KNIFE

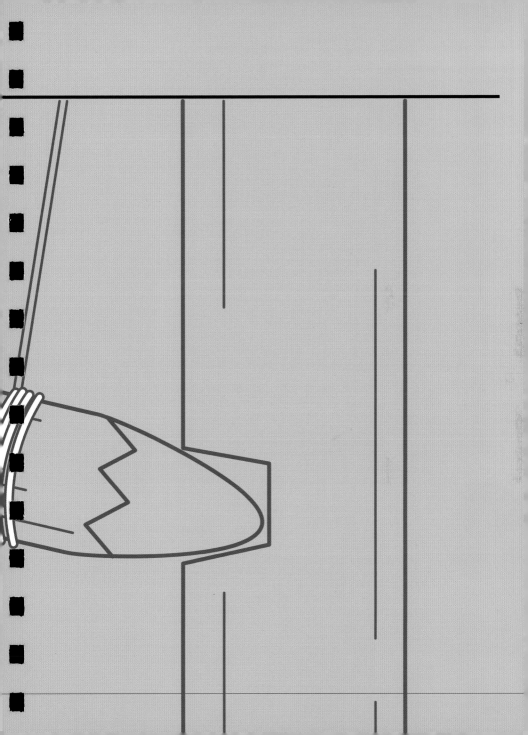

HUNTING AND GATHERING

The earliest people were hunters and gatherers, and generally successful at it, seeing as we're still here. There's no reason that you can't be too, especially since you now have command of man's earliest toolkit. In addition to your knife, you can also make use of stones more or less as you find them, and sticks either au naturel or modified to your purpose with your knife.

MAKING UP FOR LOST TIME

One thing that primitive man had over us when it came to finding sustenance in the wild was experience. Even today, children growing up in hunting-gathering societies learn by observing, practicing, and direct instruction by their elders for years before they can survive on their own. But they have millennia of experience to draw upon, where we, in general, have none. There are a lot of skills for us to catch up on.

Gathering Vegetable Foods

Calories and carbohydrates are much more important to your near-term survival than protein, which means that vegetable foods should take priority over animal foods in a survival situation. There are plenty of plant foods for the taking in most wild areas, although they vary by locale and by season. We will look at a few plants that require a knife to harvest, but it is outside the scope of this book to provide extensive lists of edible plants in your region—many of which require no tools to harvest or prepare. That information is readily available in your local library or online, and it's well worth the effort to learn about.

Catching Critters

Likewise, there are all kinds of edible insects, amphibians, and other little crawly things that can provide a lot of protein and fat for little effort. Again, refer to local resources to learn about what is safe and edible in your territory.

Fishing

There are many fishing techniques and an infinite amount of information on the subject. Simple fishing gear can be part of your emergency kit, and it can be improvised from materials in the wild. We'll look at making gear for three methods: line fishing, spear fishing, and weir fishing.

Hunting by Hand

The most seemingly straightforward way to secure meat—hunting—is the most difficult in practice. There are a few animals that you might kill with a knife, club, or thrown missile, but they won't make it easy for you.

Spear Hunting

A spear greatly increases your chances of hunting success over a knife, and should you succeed in downing something "big," like a hedgehog, you'll eat well for several meals. We'll look at a couple of techniques for hunting with spears, along with how to make them.

Trapping

Probably the most effective way to secure animal protein after fishing, trapping requires a knowledge of trap construction and siting, and a lot less patience and physical skill than hunting. We'll examine a few easy-to-make traps and snares.

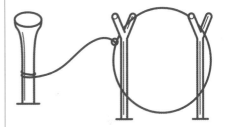

Butchering and Food Preparation

Once you've made your kill, you have to skin, clean, and butcher it, which we'll address later in this section, and then cook it, which we'll look at in the next section.

HUNTING BY HAND

A knife in the hand is of little use in securing meat, except in building traps or producing hunting tools. Most small mammals are simply too fast, too smart, or too wary to be killed by a knife thrust. Still, let's consider the options, if only to discount them before looking at more practical hunting methods.

THROWN KNIFE

On the assumption that you decided against bringing a set of throwing knives on your wilderness expedition (see page 26), your options for a thrown knife consist of your sheath knife and perhaps a pocket knife or belt folder. Let's forget the folding knives right off the bat. If you've ever tried throwing one, you know it's nearly impossible to hit a target point-first. The weight is all at the wrong end.

So that leaves the sheath knife, which is also not adequately front-weighted for throwing, but might be a little less bad for that purpose than the folder. Are you really going to risk damaging or losing your most valuable survival tool for the slim chance of securing a meal? Because really, what are your chances of hitting that rabbit?

You might argue that even if you can't reliably make the knife hit its target point-first, you still have good aim, and even if it's the butt of the knife that hits the game, he's still a goner. You're probably right. In which case, throw a rock or stick at him, and keep your knife safe for more productive things.

If you're not convinced, go outside with a sturdy sheath knife that you don't particularly value, make a rabbit-size mark at the very base of a tree, step back 20' (6m) or so, and see for yourself just how difficult it is with a stationary target.

AMBUSH

If throwing is out and we can't outrun most game, the only other way to get a knife into close proximity to living food is ambush. Knife in hand, you could stalk a rabbit run, or perhaps hide next to a gopher hole, and wait for your quarry to appear.

Well, yes. But add a few feet of reach by exchanging the knife for a spear, and you'll improve your chances considerably. If you have the patience and stealth to stalk game, there's no reason whatsoever to do it with a knife when a spear is so easy to make. (See page 74.)

RABBIT STICK

A rabbit stick is simply any stick that you throw at small game. Finally, here's a realistic approach to hunting in a survival scenario. A rabbit stick is so easy to procure that its loss is scarcely a problem. While a thrown stone might land with harder impact, a stick has the advantage of covering a wider area, making aim slightly less critical.

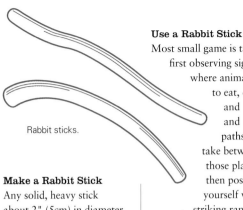

Rabbit sticks.

Make a Rabbit Stick

Any solid, heavy stick about 2" (5cm) in diameter can be a rabbit stick. One foot (30cm) is about the minimum length, and two (60cm) about the maximum. A shorter stick can be thrown faster, while a longer one reduces the need for accuracy. A stick that has a knob or a big knot at one end will have extra momentum and will spin in such a way that it can deliver a harder blow.

After cutting the stick to the length you find comfortable, smooth all its edges with your knife blade, or by rubbing it against a rock. The smoother surface will make less noise as the stick spins through the air, and so is less likely to alert the prey. If you've stripped the bark off, camouflage its unnaturally light surface by darkening it with fire, smoke, ash, or dirt.

Use a Rabbit Stick

Most small game is taken by first observing signs of where animals go to eat, drink, and sleep, and the paths they take between those places, then positioning yourself within striking range with your weapon.

When hunting in a field or meadow, a sidearm throw takes advantage of the open horizontal space. As the weapon spins horizontally, it covers a wider path, so it's more likely to hit the prey. When hunting in woods, an overhand throw is better, as it works between the trees.

As you move through woods or field, hold yourself in such a way that you can throw your weapon with little readjustment of your position. When the quarry comes into view is no time to raise your arm into a throwing position, so stalk with your throwing arm held in the ready position. Upon sighting the quarry, "wind up" only your torso slowly and gradually, arching your back backward for an overhand throw, or twisting it toward your throwing-arm side for a sidearm throw. As you throw your arm forward with all your might, use the large muscles of your torso to add power to the throw.

Overhand throw for use in woods.

Sidearm throw for fields and other open spaces.

SPEAR HUNTING

As described in the previous section, hunting with a knife is extremely difficult and unlikely to be productive, because stalking game to within arm's reach requires a degree of stealthiness that most people don't possess. What is needed is some way to strike the animal from a longer range. Since it's inadvisable to use knife throwing as a hunting technique (see page 72), let's consider the spear as a hunting weapon.

Types of Spear

Spear hunting comes in two varieties: thrusting and throwing. The typical thrusting spear is only 4–6' long (1.2–1.8m), so a great degree of stealthiness is still required, but this short standoff distance greatly increases your chances of success. A throwing spear should be 6–7' (1.8–2.1m) long and 1–1½" (2.5–3.8cm) in diameter at the larger end. With a throwing spear, the standoff is much greater—you will try to strike from distances as great as about 15' (4.6m), so it is that much easier to get within range of your game. But for reasons that will be discussed, the chances of a successful hunt are probably no greater than with a thrusting spear. A knife is the primary tool for making a spear of either type, and certain knives may also be used as spearheads in limited situations.

Making a Thrusting Spear

- Use your knife to fell a sapling of the proper size with no branches over the desired length. A thrusting spear need not be perfectly straight.

- For hunting small game (rabbits, woodchucks, etc.), a thrusting spear may simply have a sharpened end and need not have an attached head.

- Sharpen the smaller end of the shaft. The point must be as sharp as possible without being excessively delicate. Since a point's strength is influenced by variables such as the type of wood and its degree of dryness, it is not possible to recommend a specific angle for the point, so the ideal balance must be determined by trial and error.

- After you have carved the point, strengthen it by fire-hardening (see box). This drives out the moisture and turns the wood light brown, but does not blacken it.

- It's best not to strip the bark from a spear shaft, because that makes it highly visible to game. If you prefer the feel of a bare shaft, scuff it up by rubbing it with sand or a rock, and darken the wood by rubbing it with ash or browning it carefully over a fire.

BONE SPEARHEADS

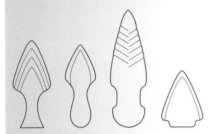

Bone—particularly fresh bone—can be carved with a sharp knife. Hold the workpiece firmly against a log or stump, and always cut away from the off hand. The area that will be held by the shaft should be fluted—flattened or even hollowed—to aid in making a secure connection. Similarly, leave a good long tang—the part of the head that will be fastened in the shaft. This should be at least as long as the exposed part of the head. You may make it exactly as wide as the shaft, so that its edges will be flush. Alternately, you may carve "ears" on its lower end, extending no farther than the widest part of the blade section. After the head is lashed to the shaft, these ears will prevent it from being pulled out.

Knives as Spearheads?

Harder and sharper than a stone or bone point, a steel knife seems to present an attractive option as a spearhead, but its practicality is actually quite limited. Only fixed-blade knives should be considered—even the most rugged lockback folder may not survive a mis-cast that strikes a rock, or a vigorous thrust that strikes bone or penetrates frozen ground. If the knife has a guard between the handle and the blade, it will limit penetration to the length of

FIRE-HARDENING WOOD

Fire-hardening can be done by holding the point over a flame, but this requires care to prevent charring. A better approach is to bury the point in dry earth or sand close to, but not in, the base of the fire. Pull it out after a few minutes to check if it's getting warm and beginning to dry. If not, place it a little closer. Continue to check periodically until it is dry, hard, and light brown.

the blade. This may be okay for small animals, but not for hunting big game or for protection against large predators. Then there's the problem of hafting the knife. You could lash it to the side of the shaft, but this will create an obstruction to easy penetration, and it will make the weapon too unbalanced for throwing. On the other hand, cutting a notch wide enough to accept a knife handle would require a pretty hefty shaft—too big for a throwing spear. Such a weapon might work for small game, but why hunt small game with a big clumsy weapon? You'd be better off with a sharpened stick, or perhaps a spear with a small bone point.

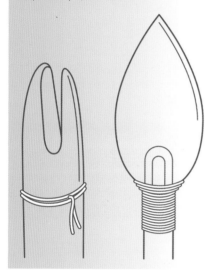

A thin spearhead can be fitted into a simple split in the end of the shaft, while a thicker head requires the shaft to be notched. With a knife, split or notch the end of the shaft in line with the point's taper, not across it.

Hunting Small Game: Thrusting Spear

The most effective hunting technique for small game is the stationary ambush. It requires a great deal of patience but not much skill, and anyone who's really determined is likely to succeed at it. The first test of patience is in locating a place for your ambush. Once you have found an appropriate spot, camouflage yourself with dirt, leaves, sticks, or grasses, and wait quietly. The best times for most animals are dawn and dusk, but any time might be productive. Some animals will instantly notice the appearance of a bush or pile of debris next to their entrance; others will ignore it if it looks natural and doesn't smell like a predator.

Having learned your quarry's movements, you know when you must be in hiding. You have camouflaged yourself and done everything you can to eliminate or cover your scent. Now comes the second test of patience: the ambush itself. Now you wait silently, with the spear held in such a way that you will be able to thrust without repositioning it or yourself, without a windup. It is harder than you think, to remain absolutely motionless, to ignore an itch or a twig digging into your cheek or your foot. When the moment is right, you will thrust hard and deep.

Some animals start forward at the first hint of danger; others may dart to one side or another. If you think the beginning of your thrust will tip off the quarry by a fraction of a second, try to compensate by "leading" the game just a little bit.

Hunting Small Game: Throwing Spear

Small game can also be hunted with a thrown spear, either from ambush or by stalking. Always stand sideways to your quarry, with your off-side arm pointing toward the target. Your throwing arm is held as far back as it can go, with the spear horizontal and the spearhead beside your own head. Lean toward your dominant side, so that that foot bears almost all your weight. Your other leg will be straight, extended forward at an angle, with the foot tipped down and only the toes against the ground.

Bring the throwing arm forward quickly, leading with your elbow. At the release, your hand will be pointing straight at the quarry, and your index finger will give the spear the final little push against the indexing groove.

Fallen branches will funnel your quarry

Position yourself behind a tree or boulder

Low, leaf-covered branches provide ideal ambush cover

Look for a brook or a margin between woods and a meadow

AMBUSH LOCATIONS

You need to find where game goes to drink, eat, or bed down. You won't find this by striding purposefully through the woods; you will find it by sitting still, hidden by bushes several feet to the side of an animal's trail, a brook, or a margin between woods and meadow where animals may come to eat. Find a spot where you can position yourself behind a tree or boulder within spear's reach of where the quarry will pass. You can improve your chances by placing an obstacle like a branch along the side of a trail to funnel the quarry right next to your place of concealment. The low, leaf-covered branches above a frequently used trail may provide the ideal ambush.

Don't take your eyes off the target for a moment during the entire motion.

I hope you didn't lash your only knife to the shaft as a spearhead, because you may need it now. If the spear struck the game but didn't kill it outright, use your knife, or else a club, to dispatch the animal quickly.

Rabbits, squirrels, and other small, wary game are hard to hit with a thrown spear under the best of circumstances, and throwing a spear accurately requires much practice. Unless you are already proficient, you'll probably be better off using the thrusting method of hunting in a survival situation.

TRAPPING

If time isn't a big issue, trapping is an easier and more reliable way to get meat than hunting. It's not a practical approach if you're making forced marches to get out of the wilderness. But if you're staying in one place and waiting for rescue, it's a good idea to set a series of traps and check them twice daily.

TYPES OF TRAPS

We'll look at two common types of traps that can be made with knives. Snares rely on cordage to capture or strangle the prey, or to snap its neck by "hanging." Deadfall traps use a heavy weight to crush the prey. Both types may use bait to attract the prey, or may rely solely on their placement along an animal's habitual runs or trails to bring the prey into the proper position for the trap to work.

PEG SNARE

1 One of the simplest of all snares is the peg snare. It is an unbaited trap, typically set up along a rabbit's run or at the entrance to the home of almost any small burrowing or denning animal. Look for narrow, well-confined places in the run where the rabbit is sure to pass and where a diversion is unlikely even should the rabbit notice something odd. Tie a noose with a loose knot that slides very easily. Its diameter should be just 2" (5cm) larger than the animal's head.

Cut two sticks with short "Y"s at the top. Point their lower ends and drive them into the ground. Support the noose at the height

of the animal's head. Carve a stout peg and drive it into the ground off to the side, and secure the fixed end of the noose to this, or tie it low on the stem of a nearby bush.

A downside of a peg snare is that the animal dies slowly by strangulation. Aside from its cruelty, this actually makes the meat taste bad. The spring snares described below use a counterweight or a bent sapling to jerk the ensnared animal off the ground, either strangling it more quickly or breaking its neck for an instantaneous death.

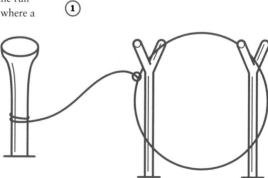

①

HOOK SNARE

2 Find a sapling that you can bend so that its top will be a few feet above an animal's run. Cut off most of the leafy branches, which would slow the speed of the spring-back. Tie a cord to the top, long enough to reach the ground when the tree is bent over.

With your knife, cut a stake with a square-topped notch near the top. Point the other end and drive it into the ground beside the run. Carve a notched trigger piece as shown, and tie it to the lower end of the cord on the sapling. Make a noose with another piece of cord, and tie it to the trigger piece as well.

Bend the sapling down and fit the notch on the trigger piece into the notch on the stake.

Support the noose with small Y-shaped sticks, as in the peg snare. Test the trigger: it should release with very little pressure in any direction. If it sticks, modify the shape of the notches or apply grease to reduce friction.

When the animal runs into the snare, its movement will release the trigger and the sapling will jerk it off its feet.

Consider setting the snare facing the side of a run, and placing bait just on the other side of the noose. The bait should be positioned so that the animal can approach it only by sticking its neck into the noose.

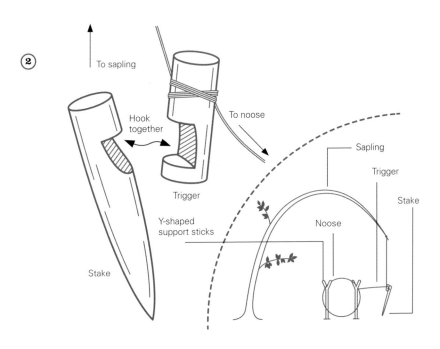

To sapling

Hook together

To noose

Trigger

Y-shaped support sticks

Stake

Sapling

Trigger

Stake

Noose

3 PLUG SNARE

With the exception of the trigger, this is identical to the peg snare. Carve a notch into a standing sapling or a heavy stake with a square top, bottom, and back. Carve a square-ended plug that will just stay in the notch when it is tied to the bent sapling. Tie the noose to the plug. Any pull on the noose should be enough to pull the plug from the notch. Adjust the fit as needed.

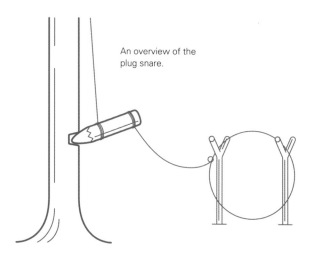

An overview of the plug snare.

③

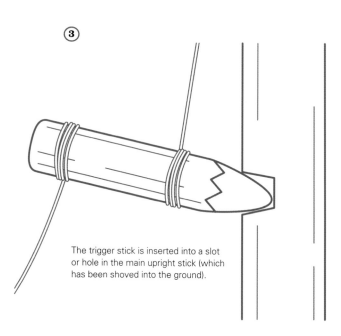

The trigger stick is inserted into a slot or hole in the main upright stick (which has been shoved into the ground).

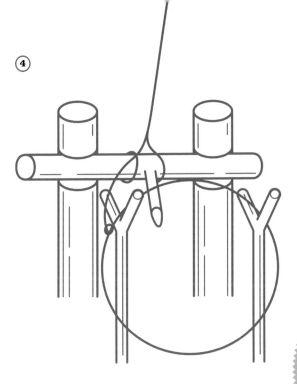

④

TIP

These snares can be adapted to catch fish by using a baited hook on the end of a line instead of a noose. In the case of the T-bar snare, a T-shaped trigger isn't needed at all: a straight bar will suffice as the tie-off for the fishing line.

4 T-BAR SNARE

This is a baited spring snare. Cut two notched stakes, as shown, and drive them into the ground. Find a piece of wood with a small branch sticking out from it at a right angle, and cut it into a T shape, with the small branch forming the vertical part of the T. Shape the horizontal ends of the T so that they can be secured in the notches by the upward pull of a sapling spring, but still release easily. Cut a barb or two on the vertical part of the T to secure your bait. Tie the noose to the T-bar, and tie the T-bar to the top of the bent sapling with a long cord. Support the noose on two Y-shaped sticks in front of the bait so that the animal must stick its head through the noose to reach it.

5 WEIGHTED BIRD SNARE

The sensitivity of this baited snare can be adjusted to suit the weight of the birds you'd like to catch. Only very light cord is required to secure anything smaller than a goose.

Bore a hole near the top of a heavy stake. Point the stake and drive it into the ground. Tie a noose and pass the tail through the hole, with the slipknot against the hole. Tie a rock to the end of the tail. Carve a light stick that will make an attractive perch for a bird, shaping the end so that it can wedge the cord in place but still be dislodged with only the slightest movement. Place the noose over the perch, and set bait on or near the perch. (Many birds that feed on the ground will first land on the perch to look over the surroundings before descending to feed.) When they settle on the perch, the stick will fall out, releasing the rock. This will pull the noose tight around the bird's legs, and pull the bird against the stake.

6 FIGURE-4 DEADFALL

This popular trap, which may be set unbaited or baited, is tricky to build but quite effective.

Drive a stake into the ground, then carve a chisel point on its top. Carve the diagonal stick, as shown, with a notch to fit over the top of the stake, and a chisel point on the lower end. Carve the horizontal stick with a notch to contain the diagonal stick's chisel point, and a second, hook-shaped notch at 90° to the first, to fit around the stake. If you will bait the trap, point the end of the horizontal stick opposite the notched end.

Holding the diagonal and horizontal sticks in position, lean a section of log against the upper end of the diagonal stick. You may need to drive stakes into the ground on one or both sides of the log to keep it from rolling off.

Any movement of the free end of the horizontal stick should spring the trap. You can place bait on the pointed end, or position the trap so that an animal will brush against it as it passes along a run or trail.

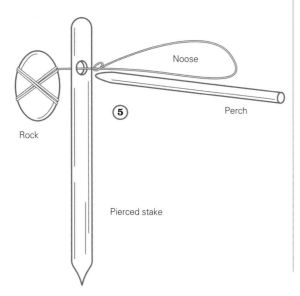

Noose

Perch

(5)

Rock

Pierced stake

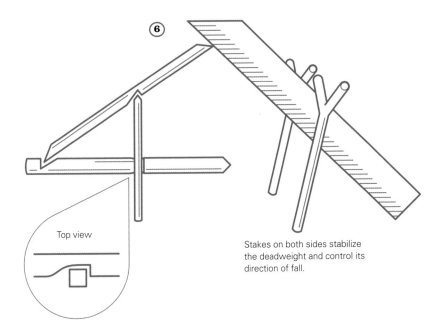

6

Top view

Stakes on both sides stabilize
the deadweight and control its
direction of fall.

7 SURVIVALIST DEADFALL

Said to be more reliable
to set up than a figure-4
deadfall, this version also
requires little or no carving.
It's really just a balancing act
with three sticks and a heavy
weight. The ground must be
quite solid, as any settling
will cause the setup to
topple. It may be set baited
or rely on incidental contact.

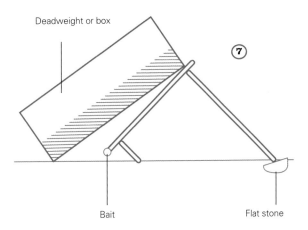

Deadweight or box

7

Bait

Flat stone

HUNTING BIG GAME

Taking big game with a thrown, improvised spear is nearly impossible unless you are hunting in a large, coordinated group capable of cornering the beast and delivering multiple spears. A single hit will rarely kill quickly, and any injured large animal—even a deer— is quite capable of injuring you back, severely. Don't even think about wild hogs or bear.

If, in spite of these warnings, you're determined to hunt deer with a spear, thrusting from an ambush is the only practical approach. Whereas any solid hit may be enough to immobilize small game sufficiently for the purposes of dispatching it, with large game you need to go for a vital organ, and you need to thrust as hard and deep as possible. Even penetrating the hide can be difficult with some animals.

You don't want to tangle with an injured deer at close range. If you've made a solid hit deep into the animal's vitals, release the spear and let it run off. It won't go far, and it will leave a trail of blood that should be easy to follow. Be extremely cautious when approaching the down animal. Until it's definitely dead, consider it dangerous.

 LIMP-TRIGGER SNARE

Here's another trigger mechanism that can be used for a bent-sapling spring snare. This one is very sensitive and it makes a good baited trap for even the smallest animals. It is tricky to set up, however, and may take some fiddling to get it to remain in the "set" position.

Carve a stake with a large, square-topped notch near the top, and drive it into the ground so that the top of the notch is about 8" (20cm) from the ground. Cut a small stick 7½" long (19cm). Cut another stick ½" (1.5cm) in diameter and 5" (13cm) long. Tie a cord from the top of the sapling to one end of the shortest stick. Pull down the sapling, place the short stick horizontally under the notch, and place the longer stick vertically under the opposite end. The upward pressure of the sapling will be resisted by the longer stick. If the longer stick

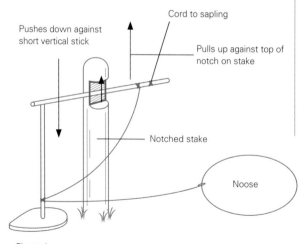

Pushes down against short vertical stick

Cord to sapling

Pulls up against top of notch on stake

Notched stake

Noose

Flat rock

sinks into the ground, place a small flat rock or slab of wood beneath it.

Tie a noose with a longer "tail" than usual. Midway down the length of the tail, tie it to the longer, vertical trigger stick. Tie the very end of the noose to either the horizontal stick or directly to the cord leading to the top of the sapling. Any disturbance of the vertical trigger will knock the horizontal stick out of position and spring the trap.

9 KEEPER SNARE

One of the problems with sapling-spring traps is that the sapling will eventually take a "set," and lose much of its springiness. Using a rock counterweight to pull the noose tight avoids this problem.

This is a very simple snare used without bait on an animal's run, under a tree that is strong enough to support your weight, as you have to climb it to set the trap. The noose requires a very long tail. Set up the noose on Y-sticks, as in the peg snare, and run the tail through a forked branch directly above it. Tie a short

A SPECIAL TECHNIQUE FOR POLAR BEARS

It is said that every Eskimo boy used to know about this trick. If you're about to be attacked by a polar bear, place the butt of the spear on the ground, set your foot on it, and angle the shaft so that the point is at the height of the bear's chest. Now stand your ground. In theory, the bear will ignore the spear and continue charging right onto its point, impaling itself deeper and deeper until he either reaches you or dies.

That's how it works in theory. Please don't put it to the test.

stick across the fork to keep the tail in place, but leave plenty of room for movement. Tie a rock to the end of the tail, and balance it gently on a branch directly above the forked branch. The rock should weigh three or four times as much as your quarry, and there should be no slack between the noose and the rock.

Any disturbance of the noose will pull the rock from its branch. As it falls below the forked branch, it will raise the noose and the animal with it.

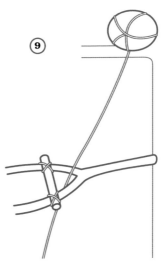

⑨

PREPARING SMALL GAME

If you haven't done it before, the idea of dressing game and butchering your own meat may make you squeamish. But if you are truly in a survival situation, and you have just killed a small animal using the improvised hunting tools or methods described in the previous chapters, you can certainly get over your misgivings and get on with it.

FIELD-DRESS A RABBIT

Fresh-killed game spoils rapidly, due to the live bacteria that remain in the stomach, intestines, and elsewhere. You want to dress or gut the animal immediately. Opening up the carcass and removing the blood and organs will cool the meat and slow spoilage. Because rabbits are common almost everywhere and are relatively easy to catch, we'll use them for our example. The procedures for most small game are similar.

Before starting, you must make absolutely sure the animal is dead. If there's any doubt,

a hard blow to the head with a club will do the job.

Skinning

The next step is skinning. Unless you have a helper to hold things steady, hang the rabbit by its hind legs from a low, sturdy branch, or lay it on the ground and tie the legs to a tree. Make an incision from one ankle down toward the crotch and back up the other leg to the opposite ankle. You can now grab the skin at the incision and back and pull it off like a glove, right over the head.

SKINNING A SQUIRREL

Squirrels don't give up their skin as easily as rabbits so don't tie them up like rabbits. Instead, cut a 2–3" (5–8cm) long slit into the skin of the back. Place two fingers of each hand in the incision and pull the skin apart sideways.

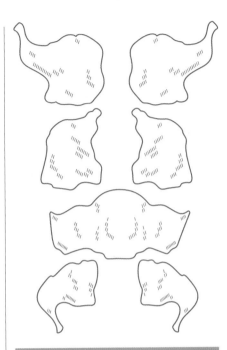

Gutting and Butchering

Untie the carcass. Cut off the head at the base of the neck, working your knife carefully between two vertebrae. Cut through the lower leg joints to remove the feet and discard them. Pinch and lift the muscle at the top of the stomach cavity and make a small incision, being careful not to penetrate the organs beneath. Continuing to pinch and pull up on the muscle, place the tip of your knife in the incision with the blade facing up, and cut down toward the groin until the stomach cavity is open. Remove the organs by hand, using your knife only if necessary to free things up. Be careful not to cut or rupture the bladder or intestines, as their contents will ruin your meat. Keep the heart, liver, and kidneys and discard the rest.

Use it All

The most nutritiously efficient way to use the animal is to make a stew. Spitting and roasting the animal loses much of its fat to the flames, and rabbits and squirrels are deficient in fat to begin with. It is difficult to open the skull cleanly in order to gain access to the brain, but you can place the entire head in the stewpot with the rest of the meat and the edible organs.

FOOD SAFETY

When preparing game, make every effort to assure the meat's safety:

- Wash your hands and tools.
- Keep dirt and insects away.
- Don't allow the animal's hide to contact the meat or body cavities.
- Avoid contaminating the meat with the animal's own urine and feces.
- Cook or preserve the meat quickly to avoid spoilage.
- If the animal appears to have been ill before you killed it, don't eat it.
- Cook the meat thoroughly to kill any pathogens.

FISHING

Fishing is often a more productive way of getting meat than hunting or trapping—a good day for a rabbit hunter may mean three or four bunnies in the bag, while a good day fishing might mean dozens of fish caught. This chapter won't teach you how to fish: there's far too much expertise available elsewhere on that subject for us to add anything to it. But let's look at how you can use your knife to assist the process.

HOOK AND LINE

As long as you have a piece of string and your knife, you can make a fishing rig.

The simplest "hook" isn't a hook at all: it's a short straight piece of bone, pointed at both ends, baited and tied in the middle to the end of the line. Called a gorge, it will lodge in a fish's mouth or stomach, although not as reliably as a hook.

A bird's wishbone is easy to convert into a proper fishhook by cutting one of the legs short and whittling down the "tab." Cut a shallow notch near the end of the longer leg to secure the line.

If bone isn't available, you can use a stick. Add a small stone sinker to counter the wood's buoyancy, tying it above the hook so that the bait rises and moves freely in the current.

SPEAR FISHING

This spear is designed to capture, rather than stab, the fish from above. Depending upon the depth of water and whether you will wade or fish from a stream bank, cut a straight stick anywhere between 4 and 12'

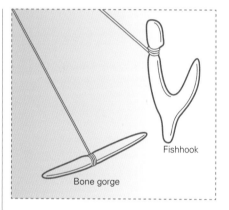

Fishhook

Bone gorge

long (1.2–3.7m) and a maximum of 1½" (3.8cm) in diameter. Sharpen the wider end, then tie a cord tightly 10" (25cm) down from the point. Split the point into four equal quarters, stopping at the cord. Sharpen the inside of the cuts, then force bits of twig into the slits so that the points splay out in all directions. You can adjust the splay according to the size of fish you're after by using twigs of different diameters, or by moving them up or down in the slits.

This spear is not designed to stab fish. It works by straddling the fish between the four points, to pin it against the bottom. Aim just

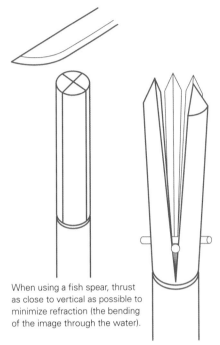

When using a fish spear, thrust as close to vertical as possible to minimize refraction (the bending of the image through the water).

behind the gills, and make sure you hold the fish down firmly. You can then reach down and grab it, or give the spear a quick twist to break its back.

WEIRS

A weir is a fish trap made of stakes, sometimes with grasses, twigs, or light branches woven between them. They can be placed across a river or stream, or across the mouth of a small tidal inlet.

The length of the stakes depends entirely on the depth of the water. Whether you use many stakes spaced close together, or weave materials between fewer, more widely spaced stakes, will depend upon the width of the stream or inlet, the availability of materials, the strength of the current, and how difficult it is to set stakes securely in the bottom.

Most fish can be guided by placing an obstruction obliquely across their path. As shown in the diagram, a funnel-shaped entrance will encourage them to enter the trap, while a wall at the other end will contain them. When fish begin finding the entrance, you can either spear them as they emerge, or place a barrier across it.

Fish can be held inside the blocked-off weir, providing a source of protein for several days.

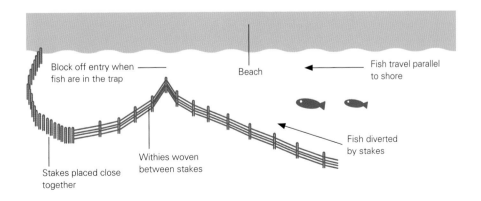

Block off entry when fish are in the trap

Beach

Fish travel parallel to shore

Stakes placed close together

Withies woven between stakes

Fish diverted by stakes

CLEANING FISH

As with small game, the way you prepare a fish can make a big difference in the amount of nutrition you obtain from it. Because many fish have a layer of fat just beneath the skin, skinning and filleting are counterproductive. In a survival situation, you want all the calories from fat you can get.

SCALING

Only fish with large, stiff scales need to be scaled before cooking. Lay the fish flat on its side and lay your knife across it at a 90° angle, with the edge facing up. Holding the fish by the tail, drag the knife forward with moderate downward pressure. If the scales catch or come off, continue dragging the back of the knife across the fish until they're all removed. If the scales are tiny and soft and the knife passes over them easily, you may leave them on.

GUTTING

At the bottom of the fish (the ventral surface), cut from just behind the gills back to the anal vent. Hold the fish open and pull out the entrails. Use a spoon or similar blunt tool to scrape the vein from below the spine. Make incisions straight down on both sides of the dorsal fin (the large fin on the back) and pull it out. Wash the fish inside and out with clean water.

OPENING SHELLFISH

Oysters, clams, and mussels are among the easiest foods to forage along the seashore. They are best opened with a blunt-ended knife, like many river-rescue knives. Your next-best option is a knife with a sheepsfoot blade. Be extra cautious when using any other blade shape, and take measures to protect your off hand, such as placing several layers of thick cloth between it and the mollusk.

TIP

Clams should first be purged of sand by placing them in a bucket of seawater overnight. If you have a handful of ground meal to throw in, that will aid the process. Change the water at least once while they soak.

1. Look carefully for a small gap between the two shell halves and insert the tip of the knife.

Examine the "front" edge (opposite the hinge) of a clam closely. You will notice a slight gap at some point, where the two halves of the shell don't fit quite so closely together. Holding the clam flat on your palm with the hinge against the heel of your off hand, work the edge of the blade carefully into this gap and press gradually but firmly until the hinge suddenly releases. Pry the upper shell back a bit and cut the two muscles holding it to the meat inside. Twist the upper shell, breaking the hinge off entirely. Cut the two remaining muscles beneath the meat. You may cook or eat raw.

2. After the blade enters, turn the point inward and twist it until the hinge releases.

To open an oyster, hold it horizontally with the flat side up and insert your blunt-point knife about ½" (1cm) beside the hinge.

Carefully work your way around the perimeter until you meet the hinge on the other side. (This is quite dangerous with a sharp-pointed knife. Although you will lose the oyster's delicious "liquor," it is much safer to hold the shell vertically on a hard surface, still protecting your hand with thick fabric.)

The rest of the process is the same as that of the clam.

3. Cutting the muscles attaching the meat to the shell will allow the shell to open fully.

VEGETABLE FOODS

Once you learn to recognize them in the wild, most vegetable foods can be gathered and processed with no tool but a basket. Of course, the available edible plants vary by region and by season. To get you started, here are a few popular choices that require a knife to harvest or prepare.

BURDOCK ROOT

A relative of the artichoke, burdock (*Arctium*) grows throughout North America, except the Deep South. The large inedible leaves (2', or 60cm long by 1', or 30cm wide) are white and fuzzy on the bottom. A central flower stalk can grow 2–9' tall (0.6–3m), but this is edible only when very small. The flower resembles that of a small thistle, and the fruits are burrs that stick to your clothing. The large taproot is the main edible part.

Harvest the root between early spring and late fall in the plant's first year (before the flower stalk appears) by simply pulling it out of the ground. Scrub off the dirt and slice it very thin, and then simmer or sauté for 20–30 minutes. It is high in carbohydrates and tastes similar to potatoes.

CATTAILS

Two species are common in wetlands throughout most of the United States: the common cattail (*Typha latifolia*), and the narrow-leaf cattail (*Typha augustifolia*). Both are edible. They grow up to 12' (4m) tall in dense stands in shallow water and muddy areas, and are easily recognized by the cigar-shape seedheads that even in spring will still be present from last year's growth. The

young shoots look like poisonous daffodil and iris shoots, but once it grows more than 3' (1m) tall, you will know it can't be the pretty flowers.

Every part is edible and nutritious. While cattails can be harvested by hand, a knife makes the job easier. After peeling back the outer layers, a knife is useful for removing the tough upper parts. Young shoots can be peeled and eaten raw or cooked: they have

with edible stems include musk thistle (*Carduus nutans*), spear thistle (*C. vulgare*), marsh thistle (*C. palustre*), cabbage thistle (*C. oleraceum*), woolly thistle (*C. eriophorum*), and cotton thistle (*Onopordum acanthium*).

Wearing leather gloves, start harvesting by cutting away the spiny leaves and branches with your knife, beginning at the top and working your way down. Scrape the blade up and down the stem to remove all the spines. Cut off the stems near the ground.

Loosen or fray the fibers away from the top end of the stem and peel them down by hand. Young stems can be eaten raw; older, tougher ones can be boiled.

a mild taste like cucumbers. The hearts are good sautéed.

PRICKLY PEAR

This cactus (*Opuntia*) is one of the signature plants of the American Southwest, easily recognized by its flat green "pads," which are topped by reddish-purple fruits from the middle of summer to late fall.

Cut pads from the plant, avoiding the spines and wearing gloves to avoid contact with the hairs. Cut out the spines and remove the hairs by wiping or burning them off or peeling the pad with a knife. Do a thorough job—although they're not dangerous, they're uncomfortable to swallow. The pads can be roasted whole or sliced and steamed. Cut the fruit in half and eat it right out of the skin. Spit out the seeds, which can cause severe gas pains.

THISTLES

Even more imposing than cactus, thistles nonetheless make good eating and are far more widespread. The stems and stalks are the most widely edible part across various species, although leaves, roots, and flower parts of some species are also edible. We'll confine our attention to the stems. Species

SURVIVING WITH A KNIFE

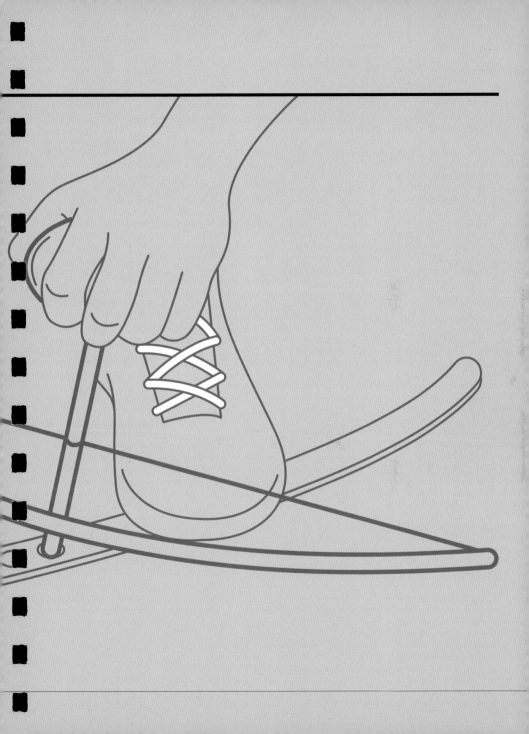

SELF-DEFENSE

If you picture using a knife to defend yourself against a dangerous animal or person, this will be the book's most disappointing chapter. You'll learn nothing at all here about knife fighting. If anything, relying on your knife to help you out of such situations makes it all the more likely that you'll get into them in the first place.

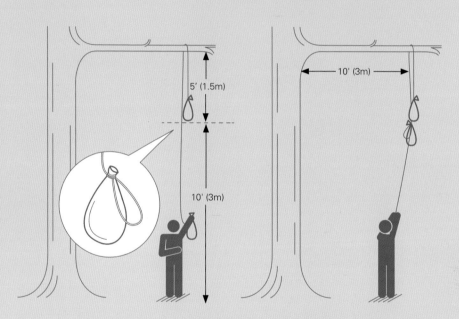

Rather than relying on your knife to protect your food from bears, hang it out of their reach. You'll both be happier with the results.

WILD ANIMALS

Simply put, the bottom line of hunting big game is: don't do it with a knife. The same goes for self-defense against bears, mountain lions, packs of wolves or any other big dangerous animals you might meet. If one of these animals were determined to kill you, your reactions and instincts wouldn't stand a chance against theirs, regardless of your knife. Luckily, death by mountain lion is about as common as being hit by meteors, and there has never been a documented case of a wolf killing a person in North America.

Bears do occasionally kill people, but, with a few exceptions, those deaths could have been easily avoided. The vast majority of bear encounters can be avoided simply by hanging your food out of their reach, and keeping it out of your shelter. If a bear enters your campsite looking for food, chase it away, banging pots and pans and even throwing rocks and sticks at it.

Black bears are timid, and in a confrontation will almost always run off if you stand tall, wave your arms, and make a lot of noise. The exception is if you have accidentally cornered them or come between a mother and her young cub. To prevent the situation from escalating, back away until you no longer represent a threat. If a black bear has already gotten into your food, don't attempt to scare it off: just back away and accept the loss. Simple, and no knife required.

Grizzly bears can be harder to discourage, but a shot of pepper spray will usually do the job. It's a good item to have in your kit if you travel in grizzly country. Even worse are polar bears, which will stalk people, and can be extremely difficult to scare off. However, anyone who finds himself on the coastal margin of the arctic wilderness has probably placed himself there intentionally and should be equipped with a gun.

WILD PEOPLE

There are dozens of books and websites devoted to knife-fighting techniques, but most of them ignore a basic reality: knife fights almost never happen. A knife attack

Black bears are generally timid and rarely a threat.

is invariably a surprise attack, which means that the person on the other end is not an opponent, but simply a victim. There is no fighting involved: just a killing. No one who wants to attack you in the wilderness with a knife will give you the slightest chance to draw your own.

You won't be cornered and forced to defend yourself or your loved ones from a crazed madman in the woods. If you're envisioning yourself in this situation, please recognize it for a dangerous fantasy and let it go. Survival depends more on avoiding trouble than overcoming it.

MAKING FIRE

Fire can be your most valuable survival tool. If you're cold or wet and have no additional clothing resources, fire will make you warm and dry your clothes. It will cook your food, signal for help, and help you make other tools. And as long as you have your knife, you can make fire.

MANY STEPS TO FIRE

As elemental as fire may be, it's not simple, and building a fire is a multi-step process. You have to:

- locate an appropriate location
- prepare the site
- gather materials for an enclosure, and assemble it
- gather or prepare three types of fire materials (tinder, kindling, and fuel wood)
- lay the fire
- kindle the flame
- build the flame
- maintain the fire

In addition, if you do not have matches, flint and steel, or some other fire-starting device, you will have to fabricate one.

FIND AND CLEAR A SPACE

To avoid attracting animals or vermin, site your cooking fire at least 200' (60m) from your sleeping shelter. Locate a clear area at least 5' (1.5m) in all directions from bushes and grass and free of overhanging trees. Seek a place sheltered from wind by trees, bushes, rocks, or

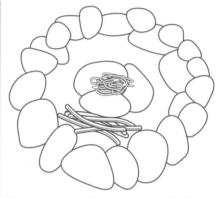

Fire ring with a small floor of stones, and kindling nearby, ready to add as soon as the tinder is alight.

a hill. A floor of rock or sand is ideal. Avoid ground that consists of a thick surface of decayed plant material. Scrape away leaves and twigs.

TIP
Fire is inherently dangerous. Follow directions for containing it. Keep young children away, and teach them safe fire habits.

THE ENCLOSURE

A fire enclosure can consist of a triangle or a ring of rocks, or two green logs at least 6" (15cm) in diameter and 1' (30cm) long. The logs, of course, may have to be replaced while the fire burns.

A floor of stones inside the ring will reflect heat up and prevent the fire from drawing moisture out of the ground.

A cooking fire need not be large. If you cut your fuel wood small, the inner diameter of a fire ring can be as small as 12–16" (30–40cm), which is more than large enough for most cooking pots. Small fires reduce the amount of fuel you must gather and prepare.

COLLECT MATERIALS

Fires must be built up in stages. The first tiny flame must take hold in fine, dry, often fluffy material called tinder. Tinder provides the heat to light slightly larger material called kindling, consisting of twigs, cones, and very small sticks. Once the kindling is alight, you can begin adding fuel wood, starting with larger sticks and working your way up to split logs.

Materials must be dry. Except in a desert, any wood lying on the ground is almost sure to be too wet to burn. Look for standing dead trees, down trees that are supported off the ground by rocks or other trees, or down trees with branches standing upright that may still be dry. Live trees may have dead branches low enough to reach. In all cases, try to break pieces off by hand or use another stick as a club to knock them down. Protect your eyes and beware of spring-back and flying chips. Anything that breaks too easily is rotten and no good for a fire.

TIP

Do not use stones from a river or lake for an enclosure. When heated, water trapped within the rock's pores will boil away, and the rapidly expanding steam can cause the rock to explode.

A fire's hunger is a surprising thing. Gather much more kindling and fuel than you think you'll need, then prepare the materials for burning. Shred tinder into fine stringy or fuzzy piles. Cut apart pine cones, and break and split twigs and sticks for a range of kindling, from the thickness of a toothpick to ¼" (6mm) in diameter. Use your knife skills (page 60) to split fire wood. A split log will take fire more easily than a whole stick of the same size.

THE VERSATILE FIRE ENCLOSURE

A fire enclosure serves many purposes. It contains the fire, concentrating the heat and preventing burning materials from escaping to where they can do damage. It shields the flame from the wind and provides rests for pots or spits.

Tinder	Kindling	Fuel Wood
fibers stripped from weed stalks	twigs	larger sticks
thistle down	pine cones	split logs
fine, dry grass	wood shavings and very thin splits	wood chunks and small logs
shredded bark from cedar, palm juniper, sagebrush	fuzz stick	
dry moss	sticks up to ¼" (6mm) diameter	
birch bark		
bird's nests		
paper		
pine needles		
leaves		

MAKE A FUZZ STICK

If good kindling is in short supply, make some fuzz sticks. Start with a stick about 1" (2.5cm) in diameter and cut thin shavings into it around the entire length, leaving them attached at the base. Make the shavings as long and thin as possible, and cut layer after layer, one beneath another. This will take fire easily, and it is excellent carving practice.

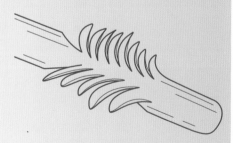

STARTING FIRES

There's a knack to starting and maintaining fires that eludes some novice outdoors-people, but becomes second nature with practice. It's a question of familiarity—if you've made enough fires, you learn to read them, to understand when they can tend themselves and when they need attention; when they need more or less fuel; more or less air. Cultivate the skill through practice: don't try to learn it in an emergency.

LAYING THE FIRE

The care with which you lay fire materials is just as important as their quality and dryness. A promising fire can peter out and die quickly if fuel and air aren't available in the right quantities.

If you have matches or a lighter, you can lay much of the fire before you apply the flame, starting with tinder, arranging light kindling around it, and being prepared to add heavier kindling and fuel wood as the fire grows. However, if you start the fire from a spark or an ember, you will have to set the tinder alight outside of the lay. In that case, the kindling must be laid so that you can place the lighted tinder within in without disturbing its arrangement.

1 Jumble Lay

A loose arrangement of the lightest kindling will work only if you can apply flame directly to the tinder below it with a match or lighter. Once the light kindling takes fire, feed it with steadily larger pieces, eventually supporting the ends on the larger side sticks

Kindling jumble-stacked on tinder

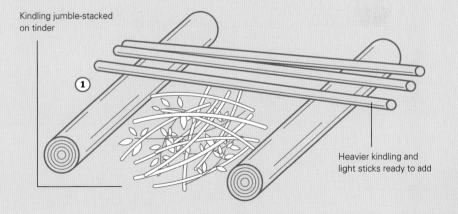

Heavier kindling and light sticks ready to add

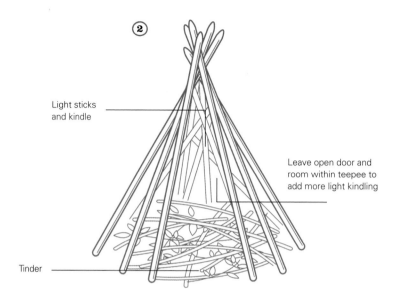

②

Light sticks and kindle

Leave open door and room within teepee to add more light kindling

Tinder

to allow it to "breathe." When you have a healthy blaze of heavy kindling going, start laying fuel wood across the side sticks, building up in a criss-cross pattern.

2 Teepee Lay

Carefully arrange the lightest kindling teepee style, leaving a "door" large enough to introduce a small bundle of burning tinder into its middle. (If you have matches, you can build the teepee around the tinder, and light it through the open door.) After the kindling takes fire, add larger kindling, laying it carefully to maintain the shape of the teepee. Work your way up gradually to small then larger fuel wood.

3 Square Lay

Like the teepee lay, the square lay can be either built around a bundle of tinder if you have a lighter, or a "door" can be left open to introduce the tinder after it's been lit outside the lay. Once the kindling is alight, build the fire up as in the other lays.

KEEPING IT GOING

After the larger fuel wood is fully alight, keeping the flame large and high is a waste of fuel. Allow it to die down until the flames are just a few inches high. At that stage, it will begin producing coals that continue burning hot for quite a long time even while the flames remain low. Feed it additional fuel only when its supply begins to run short.

Don't just toss new fuel wood on the flames: place it carefully and deliberately. Logs or splits that are too close together choke off the circulation of air and smoke and interfere with combustion. Too far apart, and the heat from the fire dissipates. At the right distance—often about 1" (2.3cm) but varying considerably with the nature of the fuel and the state of the fire—the gap between logs acts like a chimney, actively drawing air in from the bottom and out the top, promoting efficient combustion and good heat production.

TIP

Don't build a fire directly on snow or wet ground: it will draw moisture up and interfere with combustion. Instead, lay the fire on a base of stones or logs.

PUTTING IT OUT—OR NOT

The public service announcements are vociferous about extinguishing your campfire, nagging you to douse it with gallons of water and stir it like soup. That's a poor idea if you want to use the same fire ring for your next

meal. If you prepared your site and enclosure properly and wait until the flames are very small or intermittent, the fire should be able to burn down overnight without great danger. In the morning, the fire enclosure won't be a stinky sodden mess: it will likely be still warm, and you might even have live coals with which to kindle your breakfast fire.

Of course, if there is any question about the safety of the fire, err on the side of caution.

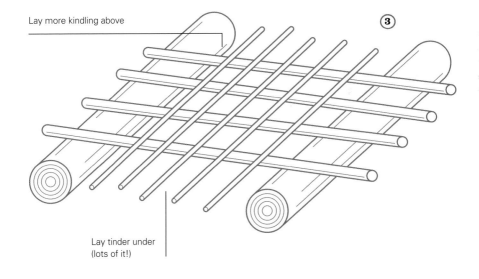

Lay more kindling above

③

Lay tinder under (lots of it!)

FIRE TOOLS

Every wilderness traveler should be equipped with multiple, redundant fire-starting devices. Pack several disposable lighters in various pockets, kits, and bags. Protect wooden matches in waterproof cases or zipper-type plastic bags and distribute them similarly throughout your gear. Finding yourself in the wilderness without an easy method to start a fire should only be the result of unforeseeable or unavoidable circumstances—something in the order of a plane crash that you survive, or the loss of your canoe and all its gear in rapids you were sure you could run safely.

FLINT AND STEEL

As long as you have your knife it's possible to start a fire from materials at hand. If you're lucky enough to be in an area of flint deposits, you have an easy method of creating a spark, by striking flint against the steel of your knife.

Tinder must be prepared with the utmost diligence to start a fire from a mere spark. Shred and fluff the materials down to its finest hairs or fibers. Roll it into a bundle, not too dense, and place it on a green leaf so that you can lift it when it's aflame. Find a place to work entirely protected from wind, and start making sparks, scraping or striking the flint with a glancing blow against the spine of your knife or vice versa, aiming the sparks toward the tinder. Soon a spark will ignite a fiber of tinder. Blow oh-so-gently to try to transfer that tiny flame to a nearby fiber, and then to another. Most such attempts will fail, but eventually you will succeed in setting the bundle aflame.

Carefully lift the leaf and transfer the bundle into your fire lay, then nurture the fire in the normal manner.

Artificial "flints" are available from survival specialty suppliers that produce a hotter spark, but it's hard to imagine a scenario in which you lose all your carefully packed lighters and matches but still have your store-bought flint-and-steel equipment, unless it's attached to your sheath.

FIRE PLOW

Rubbing two sticks together really can start a fire with this device. The hearth or fireboard can be round or flat, but it must be dry or just slightly punky softwood like cedar or poplar. Size is not important, but it must be long enough to brace under your knee while leaving the trench clear. Use your knife to start the trench: you need not carve deeply, for friction will do the rest.

FIRE PLOW

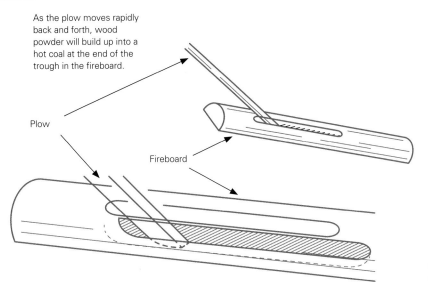

As the plow moves rapidly back and forth, wood powder will build up into a hot coal at the end of the trough in the fireboard.

Plow

Fireboard

The plow is made from similar wood, from 10–16" (25–40cm) long and 1–1.5" (2.5–4cm) in diameter. Carve a beveled end on the bottom.

As you slide the plow back and forth very rapidly, tiny bits of wood dust will begin to collect at the far end of the trench. They will be hot, due to the friction, but they will cool quickly unless you are working even faster to constantly add more hot dust to the pile. If you stroke too far, you will scatter the pile and have to start again. If you stroke too short, the dust won't collect into a hot dense ball.

When the ball begins to smoke, stop stroking and blow it gently to nurture the coal. Tip it carefully onto a green leaf and transfer it to your fire lay.

DESERT ISLAND FIRE PLOW

There's a scene in the movie *Cast Away* in which the hero, played by Tom Hanks, teaches himself to use a fire plow under desperate survival conditions. As he feverishly strokes the plow back and forth, his hand slips and he cuts himself badly on the stick's sharp upper end. It's a worthwhile lesson: smooth the edges of the plow, and work carefully to maintain control. When Hanks finally succeeds in making fire with the plow, it's one of the film's most joyous moments.

FIRE DRILL

The fire plow is quick and easy to make, but difficult to use. In contrast, the fire drill requires more time and effort to construct, but it will produce a glowing coal to start your fire more easily.

Five parts are required:

The hand socket can be of bone or hardwood. Carve or abrade a shallow round hollow on the underside.

The bow can be any strong springy branch between 14 and 24" (35–60cm) long and about ¾" (2cm) thick.

The spindle and the fireboard can be almost any wood as long as it is dry and not highly resinous, but softwoods work more quickly. The spindle is about 10" (25cm) long and 1" (2.5cm) in diameter. Its bottom is rounded and its top has a broad point. The fireboard can be any length and width, but no more than about ½" (1.2cm) thick.

A length of strong cord or leather thong. A bootlace will work, but it will wear quickly.

About ¾" (2cm) in from one edge of the fireboard, carve or abrade a shallow round recess. Then carve a V-shaped notch in the edge, with its apex intersecting the recess.

COMPONENTS OF THE FIRE DRILL

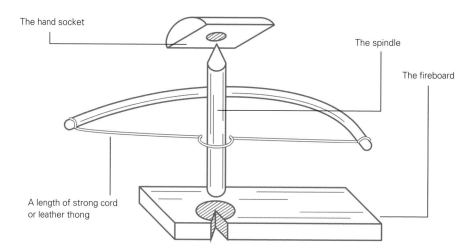

The hand socket

The spindle

The fireboard

A length of strong cord or leather thong

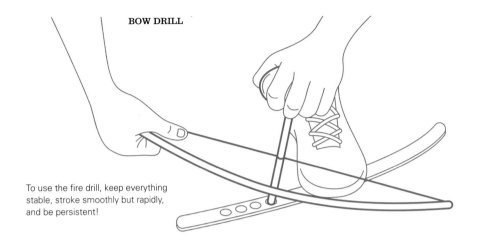

BOW DRILL

To use the fire drill, keep everything stable, stroke smoothly but rapidly, and be persistent!

Using the Bow Drill

String the bow as shown. Hold the spindle against the bowstring and give it a twist so that the string encircles the spindle. Place the lower end of the spindle in the recess of the fireboard. Hold the socket in your off hand against the top of the spindle. Grab the bow in your primary hand. Use your foot or knee to hold the fireboard steady on the ground. Place a green leaf beneath the notch.

Pressing down moderately with the hand socket, "saw" back and forth rapidly with the bow, spinning the spindle. If it doesn't turn easily, adjust the tension of the bow, reduce pressure on the socket, or smooth or lubricate the top of the spindle. When you get it right, you'll be able to feel the spindle steadily but gently abrading the fireboard as you saw.

It's all too easy to lose control of the spindle and have it pop out of the socket. To avoid this, brace the part that has the socket against the shin of the leg that's holding down the fireboard, to keep the top of the spindle perfectly stationary. Concentrate on keeping your bow strokes level and regular, maintaining the bowstring in the middle of the spindle.

Hot wood dust will begin to collect in the notch. Continue sawing until the dust accumulates into a coal that fills the notch. Gently slip the coal out on the leaf and transfer it to your fire lay.

COOKING METHODS

Now that the fire's going, it's time to start cooking. It's an easy matter to rest a pot or pan between two logs or three stones, but if you've lost your cooking gear, your knife can help you out of a bind once again.

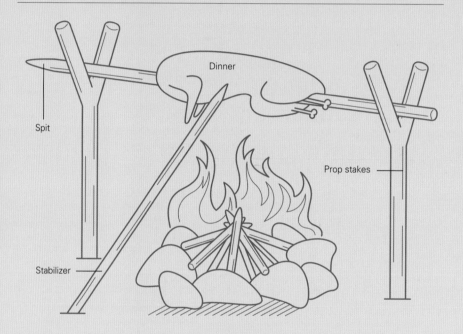

Dinner

Spit

Prop stakes

Stabilizer

SPIT

Small mammals are often cooked on a spit, but even a squirrel takes a while to cook, and it's no fun trying to hold one steady over a fire the whole time.

To support the spit, cut two stakes with Y-shaped tops and pound them into the ground on either side of the fire. If you find

that the meat keeps flopping over into the same position when you turn the spit, cut a long, light stick and sharpen one end to stabilize the meat, as shown.

POT HANGER

If you haven't lost your cooking gear, a pole stretched across a pair of Y-stakes can also be used as a pot hanger. If you make the stakes just a bit taller, it's a nice way to keep a pot of water warm for tea while you laze around the fire after a meal.

Pot hanger—high above flame to just keep the tea water warm

COOKING RACK

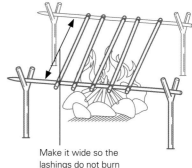

Make it wide so the lashings do not burn

FISH GRILL

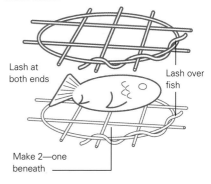

Lash at both ends

Lash over fish

Make 2—one beneath

RACK

Building a wooden rack over a fire isn't as crazy as it seems at first glance. If you use green wood at least 2" (5cm) in diameter and place it just above the live flames, it will last for well over an hour—long enough to cook two or three meals. Or build it even higher and use it to smoke your meat to preserve it for long-term use.

TIP
Another pot-free cooking method is hot-rock cooking in a bark container. See page 126 for details.

FISH GRILL

Many fish will simply fall apart as they cook. To prevent your hard-won meat from falling into the fire, make a fish grill out of young green branches. Make two rectangles or ovals, and weave a wide mesh of green branches with a simple over-under-over pattern. Tie the two pieces together over the fish and rest the grill on stones over a low fire or hot coals.

FIRE FOR COMFORT

All by itself, fire does a surprisingly poor job of keeping you warm on a cold night. True, it can make one side of you as warm as you can stand, but your opposite side remains exposed to the frigid air. Here are some tricks to improve the situation.

1 REFLECTED HEAT
The problem with an open fire is that you're only on one side of it, while its heat is radiating in all directions, including up. You can reflect some of that heat in your direction by building the fire against a boulder, or by building a "wind block" behind it (see page 115).

That still leaves your back out in the cold, but another barrier behind you will reflect some of the heat that goes by and send it back where it's needed. By the same principle, a fire placed close in front of your lean-to (but not so close as to be a danger) will warm you from both front and back.

2 CONDUCTIVE HEAT
If you have no shelter, hot stones can make a wonderfully toasty bed on a cold night. Dig a bed-sized trench 15–18" (38–46cm) deep. Collect enough stones 6–8" (15–20cm) in diameter so that, when spaced about 6" (15cm) apart, they cover the area of your bed. Lay a fire to cover the trench and light it. Keep it going for at least an hour, then knock it apart and carefully move the wood to your cooking fire enclosure. Cover the stones with sand or dry soil, and lay grass, leaves, or other soft bedding material on top of it. The stones will radiate heat for many hours.

To conserve firewood, heat the stones in a smaller fire then transfer them into the trench with tongs (see page 128).

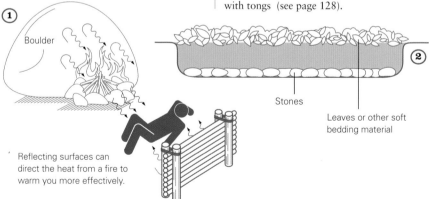

Boulder

Reflecting surfaces can direct the heat from a fire to warm you more effectively.

Stones

Leaves or other soft bedding material

SIGNALING FOR HELP

Getting rescued is usually the best response to being lost, whereas walking in hopes of finding your way is likely to get you only more lost, and if a search party is looking for you, you'll be harder to find if you're on the move. But if you stay in one place and maximize your visibility, you'll increase the odds of rescue.

CALLING ATTENTION TO YOURSELF

Signals for help may be sent by visual, audible, and electronic means. If you have a working satellite phone or a personal locator beacon, you're all set. Likewise if you know that a search party is near and you have a whistle or a gun. If neither of those scenarios apply, you'll have to rely on visible signals to catch the eye of a searcher on a far mountain peak, overhead in an airplane, or on a boat offshore of your otherwise deserted island.

FIRE AND SMOKE

Your fire-making skills (see pages 98–107) will come in handy. At night, a fire is impossible to miss, and a set of three fires in a triangle is a recognized distress signal. In order to save fuel, you might want to keep one burning at all times, and be prepared to light the other two at a moment's notice at the sound of an airplane. The downside to that strategy is that you might not hear the plane in time, if at all.

However, plane searches are generally made during daylight, when fire is not highly visible, whereas smoke is. Place live green leaves or moist grass on a vigorous fire to make smoke.

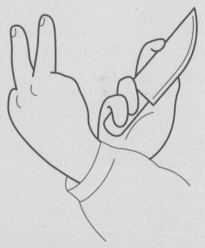

Use your fingers like a gunsight to aim reflected sunlight toward a distant search party.

REFLECTED LIGHT

Searchers can also be attracted by reflected light. Before you leave home, turn your knife blade into a signaling mirror by buffing it on a cloth wheel with polishing compound. (Not all knife steel will take the required polish.) A large, wide blade works best for this purpose.

It's necessary to shine the sunlight directly at the searcher. At a great distance, you won't be able to see the glint of the reflection against

SEARCH PARTIES

Search parties are usually called into action by folks on the "outside" who know that someone has gone missing. Any time you head into the wilderness, make sure someone knows where you'll be and when you plan to emerge. Leave explicit instructions about what authorities to contact and when. You may not want them calling out the hounds if you were simply delayed for a day.

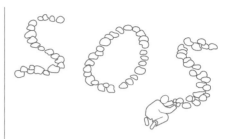

The bigger the sign, the better the chances someone will see it from the air.

your target, but you can aim it in the right direction nonetheless. Hold your off hand at arm's length and frame the target between two fingers, like a target in a gunsight. Position the knife so that sunlight reflects on your fingers, then tilt it back and forth or up and down, keeping the glint of light moving between the fingers. Especially if the searcher is between the sun and you, he or she should get the message. If the searcher is in an airplane, keep flashing until he or she has clearly identified your exact location.

GROUND SIGNALS

Another approach to being found from the air during daylight is to leave patterns on the ground. Tarps, tents, or clothing draped over bushes may be easily visible, but you can send more explicit messages by creating specific patterns, as shown. Ground signals may be made from sticks or logs, rocks, or by trampling patterns in sand or snow. If you're on the move, leaving arrow signals indicating your direction of travel will help searchers find you.

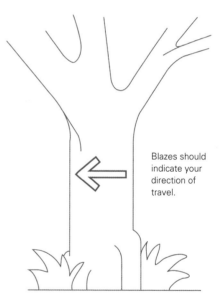

Blazes should indicate your direction of travel.

MAKING CAMP

While you're waiting for rescue, making a proper camp will provide you with essential shelter, make you more visible, and keep you occupied. Once settled, you'll be able to devote time to foraging, setting a trapline, or simply making yourself more comfortable. The first step is to choose your location; the next is to provide yourself with shelter.

SHELTER CHOICES

Shelter is needed for protection against rain or snow, cold, or excessive sunlight. The type of shelter you build will depend upon the materials available, the severity of the weather, and the degree of permanence desired. We'll look at these shelters in the following pages:

Debris Hut: a simple shelter made of sticks and insulated with leaves, for protection against cold, with partial rain protection. Quick and easy to build.

Shade Shelter: teepee-shaped but only partially covered with sticks. Quick and easy to build.

Wind Block: A solid wall of timber to protect you from cold breeze, when precipitation isn't a problem.

Squirrel Nest: The simplest of all shelters, a pile of leaves is surprisingly effective at providing warmth and rain protection.

Lean-To: a structure of sticks that may be covered by a wide variety of materials, for protection against rain and wind. Ease of build varies from quick and easy to relatively involved.

Wickiup: teepee-shaped hut made from sticks and covered with thatching, for protection against cold, rain, wind, and sun. Relatively involved to build.

Quinzhee: a cave carved into a pile of snow, this winter shelter is much easier to build than an igloo.

Thatched Hut: A domed or vaulted structure made from sticks and covered with thatching, for protection against cold, rain, wind and sun. Very involved and time-consuming to build.

PICK YOUR SITE

A good camp location provides proximity to resources, safety, visibility, and comfort. Here are some of the variables to consider:

1. Availability of Resources: Wood for shelter and fire are of great importance, but also consider the availability of game, forage food, and materials for producing cordage and tools.

2. Water Proximity: Choose a site close enough to a water source so that fetching drinking water isn't a big chore. But be aware of water bodies that are used by animals. You don't want to be so close that you scare away potential sources of meat.

3. Wind: A site that is open to the wind can be cold, and may make fire building more difficult. On the other hand, a steady breeze can be an advantage in hot weather, and may keep the area free of mosquitoes. Obviously, the top of a hill will usually be windier than its base, but wind can do unexpected things, and seemingly protected areas might be windy.

4. Widowmakers: Before you decide on the location of your hut or fire ring, look up. Examine the trees carefully for dead branches that might fall during high winds.

5. Flash Flooding: Dry canyons may be subject to flash flooding even in fine weather due to rainfall many miles away. Before setting up camp in a gorge or canyon, look for signs of previous flooding, such as piles of sticks or high-water marks on rock walls.

6. Visibility: If you hope to be rescued, site your camp in a clearing so that it will be visible from the air.

CAMPSITE LOCATION CONSIDERATIONS

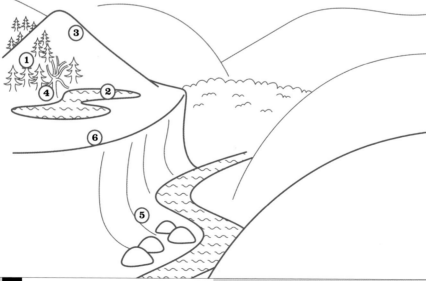

BUILDING SHELTER

How quickly do you need to build a shelter, and how long will you live in it? Ask yourself these questions when deciding between various shelter types. In a true survival situation, you probably need a shelter right away—before night falls. After you've satisfied the immediate need, begin work on a more elaborate shelter if you anticipate a long stay.

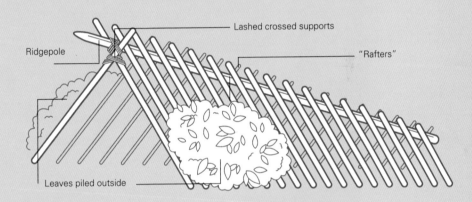

Lashed crossed supports

Ridgepole

"Rafters"

Leaves piled outside

DEBRIS HUT

This structure provides a quick sleeping shelter for one or two people. It's not possible to do anything else in it—certainly not cook.

Cut a strong straight branch at least 10' (3m) long for the ridgepole. One end goes on the ground while the other is supported by a pair of sturdy sticks set into the ground and crossed and tied near the top. If you can find a naturally occurring

support for the open end, such as a low tree limb, by all means use it. Lash the ridgepole to the support with cord or natural materials such as withies.

TIP
Build the debris hut over a big pile of leaves to avoid having to stuff it later.

Cut a bunch of sticks at least 1" (2.5cm) in diameter, and place them diagonally against both sides of the ridgepole, spacing them about 2" (5cm) apart. It is not necessary to tie them in place. Lie down inside and make sure it covers your whole body, with enough height for your toes and at least 3" (8cm) extra width on each side of your shoulders.

Begin piling leaves over the sticks and don't stop until the pile is ridiculously high. The leaves will settle quickly, and the thicker the covering remains, the better it will protect you from rain and heat loss. Lay more sticks or leafy branches over the leaves to hold them in place.

Stuff the inside of the hut with leaves for insulation, pushing them in through the door. Leave a good pile of leaves right by the door. After you wriggle in feet-first for the night, pull the loose pile of leaves in after you to close the entrance and prevent heat loss around your head.

1 SHADE SHELTER

It is not only desert travelers who must beware of an overdose of sunshine, which can lead to deadly heat stroke. Those stranded in winter environments may also need shade to protect themselves against sunburn or snow blindness.

If rain protection is not an objective, then even a bare pile of sticks will suffice for a shade shelter that resembles a partial teepee. Cut three long poles and lash them not too tightly at least 1' (30cm) down from one end. Stand the assembly upright, then spread the legs into a tripod. Take more long poles and align them between two of the poles, resting their tops in the crotch of the main poles at the top. For protection from the sun from two directions, fill in two sides of the pyramid. If long sticks are difficult to come by, lash a couple of shorter sticks horizontally between

two main uprights. You can then pile shorter sticks or even sagebrush against them. For sun protection from dawn to dusk, use four poles for the main structure and cover three sides, leaving the open side facing north in the northern hemisphere, south in the southern.

1

Lean long sticks for shade or lash many cross-pieces as needed to support piled brush.

Dig bases into earth

2 WIND BLOCK

It rarely makes sense to build a shelter to protect yourself from wind only. For the amount of work required, you might as well build a shelter that also conserves body heat and protects you from rain or snow.

Fires, however, can benefit greatly from a wind shelter. A wind block makes a fire easier to light, easier to cook on, and easier to maintain, because it will consume less fuel. A wind block also acts as a heat reflector and can be used to warm the air on the opposite side of the fire for more comfortable sleeping in cold weather.

A boulder makes an excellent wind block and heat reflector, and it absorbs and radiates it back long after the fire is out.. You can also build a wind block with sections of straight cut branches, as shown.

A windbreak can be used to shelter yourself or your fire from the wind, and to reflect the fire's heat.

SQUIRREL NESTS

The simplest of all woodland shelters is the squirrel nest. Really nothing but a big pile of leaves, it can be surprisingly effective at keeping you warm, and even dry, if you mound up a huge pile, dig yourself a trough in the middle, lie down, and then pull the leaves over you. Two or more feet (>60cm) of leaves on top will resist moderate rain for hours, but it's necessary to lie very still to keep them in place. You can improve the stability of a squirrel nest by positioning it between two fallen logs.

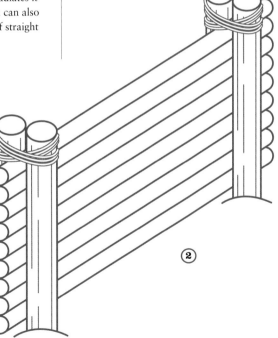

②

3 LEAN-TO

Lean-tos are a class of shelter with a common configuration but no set structure. They all consist of a flat slanted roof and, usually, two or more stout poles that serve as rafters. But how those poles are supported, and how they are covered, varies with the materials available.

TIP

For greater protection, sides can be added to a lean-to using the same methods. Ultimately, you can even enclose part or all of the front as well for a structure that will conserve heat as well as provide rain and wind protection.

If you can find a convenient boulder, low tree limb, or other ready-made support for the upper ends of the poles, by all means use it. If not, cut a pair of stout stakes, preferably Y-shaped at the top, and drive them into the ground. The apex of the Y will define the lean-to's maximum height, so plan accordingly. In an extreme situation, it need only be high enough to lie down beneath. But it can also be made high enough to sit upright and even cook beneath.

Place a very strong pole across the two uprights, then lash two more strong poles to the ridge, just inside the uprights and angling down to the ground. The material available for rain protection will dictate how many intermediate poles are needed to support the roof, and how closely they must be spaced.

4 WIKIUP

A wikiup is a teepee-shaped structure with thatching for rain protection. Start by assembling a tripod, as in the shade shelter (page 116), then dig their bases 3" (7.5cm or more) into the ground. Lean at least one

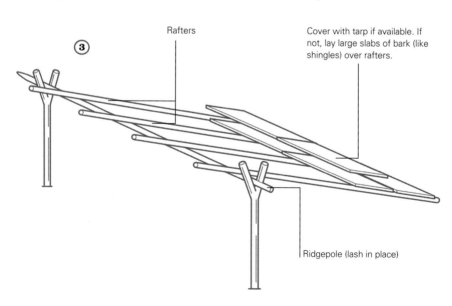

③

Rafters

Cover with tarp if available. If not, lay large slabs of bark (like shingles) over rafters.

Ridgepole (lash in place)

COVERING YOUR LEAN-TO

- Large slabs of bark can be pulled off of down, rotten trees, and these make excellent roofing material. Lay a course across the bottom, then work your way up, overlapping each course like shingles.
- Of course, if you have a tarp, use it.
- Pile several feet of leaves over closely spaced roof poles and hold them in place with light branches, as for a debris hut.
- The roof must be pitched steeply—at least 45°—if thatching is to be used (see page 121).

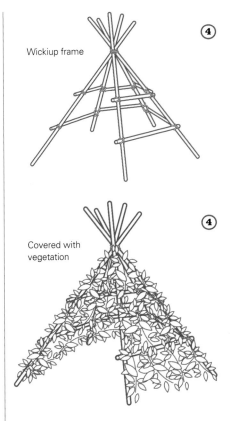

Wickiup frame

④

Covered with vegetation

④

additional upright between each of the main legs of the tripod, angling them out so that the bases of all the poles form a circle.

Lash two or three sticks horizontally between each pair of adjacent uprights, spacing the horizontals 12–18" (30–45cm) apart. You can use long flexible sticks to bridge across many uprights at once.

You will need an immense amount of grass to thatch the shelter. Rather than pulling it out of the ground by the roots, use your knife like a sickle and cut it off close to the ground. Lay the handfuls of grass in a neat row, all facing the same direction.

Take a handful of grass and tie it together as the base, leaving several inches of "tail" on the tie. It is unlikely that you will have enough string, so you will have to improvise. Some grasses can be used themselves as the tie. Other options include young shoots of various plants, split roots of certain trees, and fibers extracted from various leaves and

bark. (See page 127.) Tie the tail to one of the lowest horizontal sticks. Continue tying grass bundles close to one another on the lowest horizontal, working all the way around but leaving a space open for the door.

Repeat the process at the next level, making sure that the grass bundles overlap the first tier by 6" (15cm) or more. Continue until the entire structure is thatched. No amount of grass bundles can be considered too many: every additional one will add to the wikiup's rain resistance.

LAZY MAN'S IGLOO

True igloos require just the right snow conditions and much skill to build. If you have not practiced, any attempt to build one in an emergency will probably fail, thereby wasting time and energy. But this snow shelter, known as a quinzhee, is easier to build from nearly any snow you can move—even newly fallen snow that would be worthless for a proper igloo.

Pile up a mound of snow at least 10' (3m) long and 5' (1.5m) wide and high. If it's powdery, make the pile much higher and wait an hour or more for it to settle. Cut a dozen or so small sticks about 12" long (30cm) and stick them

into the pile all around, their ends flush with the surface. Begin excavating the mound at one end, digging like a dog and shoveling snow out between your legs until you fit inside. Carefully thin the roof, stopping when you expose the ends of the sticks. The hollow should be long enough to lie down in and tall enough to sit or kneel. Make two air passages 4" (10cm) in diameter on opposite sides, one nearly vertical and one nearly horizontal. Keep them clear to avoid suffocation.

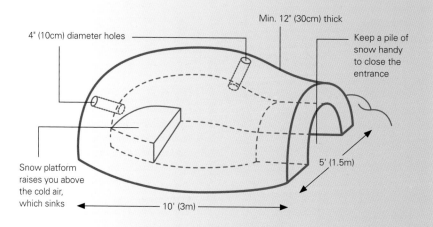

4" (10cm) diameter holes

Min. 12" (30cm) thick

Keep a pile of snow handy to close the entrance

Snow platform raises you above the cold air, which sinks

10' (3m)

5' (1.5m)

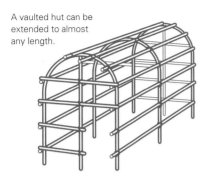

A vaulted hut can be extended to almost any length.

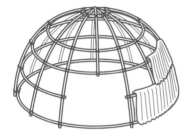

A dome hut makes efficient use of materials and is easier to heat.

THATCHED HUT

If you're in it for the long term, a thatched hut will provide you with spacious shelter for sleeping, working, and possibly even cooking. Avoid making it bigger than you need, however, for a larger shelter is more difficult to keep warm.

Thatched huts may be dome-shaped or vault-shaped, but their construction is similar. (Eastern American Indians called these wigwams and longhouses, respectively, and generally covered them with bark or hides, not thatching.) Both are supported by arches.

Cut a pair of saplings, strip them of their branches, and tie their tops together in opposite directions, overlapping the ends by 3' (1m) or more. Pound a heavy stake into the ground at least 12" (30cm) deep, leaving the same amount exposed. You may draw the stake out and place one of the sapling ends in the hole, or leave the stake in the ground and lash the sapling to it. Bend the lashed saplings into an arch and fasten the other end to the ground in the same manner.

If building a dome, set up additional arches in a circle, each new one resting on top of the one previous at the center and their bases spaced 18–24" (45–60cm) apart. If building a vault, place the arches 2–3' (60–90cm) apart. Tie horizontal cross-pieces between the arches as in a wikiup. Thatch as described for the wikiup, or use one of the following methods:

Bent Thatch

Use very long grass, cattail stalks, or similar material. Bend the material in half and drape it over the horizontals. An additional horizontal brace low to the ground is needed to keep the bottom row of thatch outside your home.

Pinched Thatch

Split a long straight stick. Lay one half on the ground, flat side up, and place cut cattails over it with the thick ends extending 6–12" (15–30cm). Place the other half over the cattails and lash or peg the two halves together every 12–24" (30–60cm). Tie this section of thatching to a horizontal brace on the shelter. Finish the first level of the wall in this manner, then repeat for the next level, overlapping the first by at least 12" (30cm).

BENT THATCH

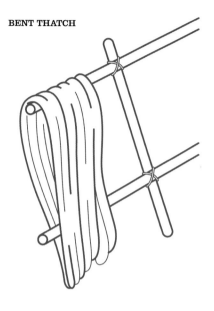

PINCHED THATCH

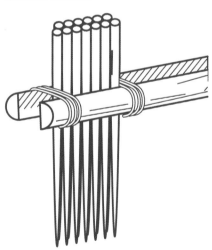

Fire represents a real danger in a thatched hut, but with due caution you might still consider it in severe weather. Here are a few pointers to help ensure that you build a fire only when it is safe to do so:

- Don't build a fire in a hut less than 6' (2m) tall.

- Place the fire under the tallest part of the roof.

- Don't place the fire between the door and a sleeping or working area.

- In a dome shelter, a smoke hole 12" (30cm) in diameter should be directly over the fire. Mix mud or clay with water into a thick slurry and "paint" several coats of it onto the thatch for at least 12" (30cm) beyond the edges of the smoke hole.

- Instead of a smoke hole above the fire, a longhouse can use openings of at least one square foot (90cm²) under both gable ends. The latter arrangement keeps rain from falling directly on the fire. Although some smoke may gather near the roof, ventilation between the two openings should prevent it from becoming too great a nuisance.

- Make sure that at least a little cold air can enter through the door to set up vertical convection currents.

- Keep the fire small.

- Be extremely vigilant about keeping loose flammable materials away from the fire.

CAMP COMFORT

The notion of seeking comfort in a survival situation is not as illogical as it may sound. The connection between staying warm and dry and staying alive is obvious, but what about a good night's sleep? The better rested you are, the better you will be able to cope with emergencies, and the more productive your work will be. And if you are waiting to be rescued, why not make it as pleasant as possible?

GRASS MAT

A woven mat can serve as a pad or a blanket for your bed, and two mats stitched together, with grass stuffing, will provide good insulation. If made from cattail stalks, mats can be used as a shelter covering. With just a bit of ingenuity, a mat can be turned into a poncho.

Mats can be woven from long grass, cattail leaves or stalks, or green, flexible reeds. Grass or thin reeds need no preparation. Cut cattail stalks or wide reeds lengthwise into strips.

Starting Narrow

Rather than attempting to weave the full width of a wide mat in one step, start with a narrow section. Lay one stalk or strand on a flat, dry piece of ground, then lay five or seven stalks at right angles to it, starting in the center of the first piece, and placing them alternating above and below. (This assumes the use of stalks or reeds. For grass, use twisted bundles.) The first strand is the beginning of the woof—the sideways part of the weave. The parallel strands are the beginning of the warp—the lengthwise part of the weave. The distance between the warps should be two or three times the width of the strands. Even them up so the woof is about 1' (30cm) from their ends.

Work in a second strand of woof, going under-over-under the opposite sides of the warp from the first, then a third, again weaving on the opposite sides from the previous row. You'll have to hold things down and straighten them out a lot, but after the third or fourth strand of woof is in place, things will begin to hold together by themselves. Use your fingertips to push the woof strands close against each other, and continue weaving in strands of woof to within a few inches of the opposite end.

Going Wide

So far, you have woven a section only a few inches wide. Now begin weaving in additional width of warp. Starting on one side, take all of the woof strands that are below the outermost strand of warp and bend upward to 90° or further. You can now lay a long strand of warp in the intersection between the upper and lower woof strands. Bend the woof strands down over the new piece of warp, then bend up all of the other woof strands and place a new piece of warp in the intersection. Continue the process until the

WEAVING MAT
1ST STEP

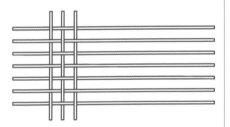

WEAVING MAT
2ND STEP

WEAVING MAT
3RD STEP

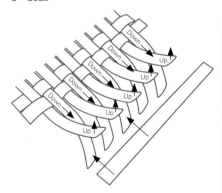

MAKE A BACKREST

If the ground is dry, take your ease sitting around the campfire with this simple backrest.

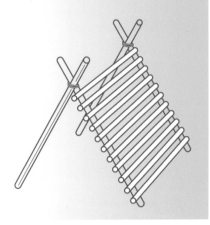

insertion of a warp brings you to within 6" (15cm) of the end of the woof. Bend the woof 180° around the last warp, then take the end and weave it back into the mat for a secure edge. Do the same thing at the ends of the warp.

To make a mat longer or wider than your materials, simply overlap strands by 8–12" (20–30cm) as you weave.

COMFY BEDS

Don't lie down, much less try to sleep, if the ground is wet or cold. Both conditions will sap body heat rapidly. Almost anything you can place between you and wet or cold ground will help—even a bed of twigs. Break or cut a great number of twigs, as long as possible, and place more beneath your torso than your legs. It won't be truly

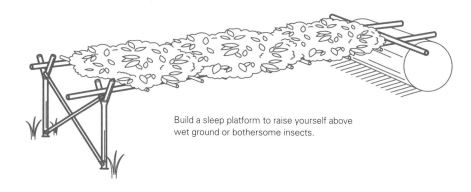

Build a sleep platform to raise yourself above wet ground or bothersome insects.

comfortable, but it's better than lying in a puddle. You can improve it by adding padding in the form of dry leaves, grass, or pine or fir boughs.

With some effort, your wood-cutting skills can produce a more comfortable bed as shown. Make the cross-pieces of the platform as straight and consistent in size as possible, and cover them with padding as for a twig bed. This has the added advantage of placing you out of reach of crawling, stinging things on the ground and, if it is built in an enclosed shelter, it raises you above the cold air, which settles at ground level.

WORKING WITH BARK

The white or paper birch (*Betula papyrifera*) grows across much of northern North America. Should you be "lucky" enough to be stranded within its range, you will find its bark to be a valuable resource, capable of being turned into a spear sheath, all manner of baskets and containers, and even canoes (see page 148). This container can be used as a cooking vessel or as a basket for collecting berries or nuts.

Harvesting Birch Bark

Birch bark is most easily removed from the tree in May and June. With more work, it can be harvested throughout the year, but only with difficulty in winter. With the tip of your knife, make a vertical cut the length of the piece you need. If the width is to be the tree's circumference, cut all the way around the trunk at the top and bottom of the vertical cut. If you need only a part of that, make a second vertical cut and connect the two with horizontal cuts. Use a wooden wedge to begin peeling the bark from the tree. There are two layers of bark: you need only the outer, more papery layer. If you remove the inner spongy layer all the way around, you will kill the tree.

When the bark is free along the entire height of the vertical cut, you may be able to simply peel it off with your hands. If not, continue using the wedge to separate it from the inner bark bit by bit. If it still won't come, boiling water will help loosen it up. Once it's off, use it promptly or keep it submerged in water to prevent it from drying out.

A COOKING CONTAINER

This is one of many container styles possible. Because it has no seams, it works well as a cooking container. If you've lost your pots and pans, it can be a life-saver—or at least a meal-saver.

1. Use the inner surface of the bark for the inner surface of the container.

2. To make the folds, heat the bark over a fire as hot as you can handle, then crease it quickly.

TIP

The simplest of forks can be carved from a forked twig. You'll find that you don't need more than two tines. A spoon requires a wider piece of wood and more whittling, but you'll need it to eat the stew

3. To hold the creases in place, poke a hole through all three layers of folded bark and tie it with a narrow strip of bark or a bit of split spruce root. Alternately, carve four clothespin-like clamps from wood to secure the creases.

To cook in a bark container, heat rocks in the fire, lift them with tongs (see page 130), and place them in water in the container. Avoid placing the rocks in direct contact with the bark: make sure they rest on sticks or leaves. When the rocks have transferred most of their heat, pull them and replace them with more hot rocks.

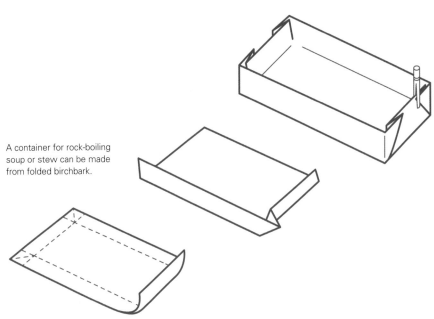

A container for rock-boiling soup or stew can be made from folded birchbark.

CORDAGE

Any trip into the wilderness should be equipped with a variety of cordage, ranging from fishing line to climbing rope. But in a long-term survival situation, it is unlikely that you'll have enough cordage to build shelters, make snares, and perform the dozens of other tasks for which it is needed. Luckily, materials from which cordage can be made are likely at hand.

SOURCES OF FIBER

Here are some of the more readily available sources of fiber for cordage:

 Basswood: This tree (genus *Tilia*) is known as either basswood or linden in North America, and as lime in Britain. Make a horizontal cut 4–6" (10–15cm) wide near the base of the tree and pry upward until you can grab the end. Hold it firmly while walking backward, "zipping" a long strip of bark upward until it narrows to a point and drops off.

 Cattail: Both leaves and stalks are easily harvested with a knife.

 Grasses: Most long grasses are best harvested in the fall, just after they die.

 Milkweed, dogbane: Pound the stems, then slice them lengthwise and pull out the material inside, leaving the outer fibers intact.

 Rose: Scrape off the thorns and outer bark and discard. Peel off the inner bark for use.

 Thistle: The outer bark is usable for cordage.

 Yucca, agave: Both yield excellent fiber from inside the meaty leaves. Pound them with a club against a rock, use water to wash the pulpy meat away, and repeat until only the fibers remain.

OTHER TYING MATERIALS

When a lashing does not require fine flexible cordage, other materials that require virtually no preparation may be used. The roots of black and white spruce trees are easily harvested and quite flexible. Dig around the base of the tree and find a root no thicker than your little finger. Cut it free, then simply pull it out of the ground. It is not unusual to obtain lengths of 20' (6m) or more.

SPINNING CORDAGE

The amount of effort required to spin cordage by hand varies greatly according to your requirements. Cordage for building structures or tying thatching to a hut can be rough and may be produced quickly. Snares require a bit more attention, and fishing line and bowstrings must be made with care.

Hold a small bundle of fibers between the thumb and index or middle finger of both hands. Twist both ends clockwise until the bundle kinks in the middle, causing both ends of the bundle to face in the same direction. Secure the kink to a solid object with a bit of cord. Continue twisting the two ends clockwise between your fingers while passing them counterclockwise around each other.

Before you reach the end of the fibers in the first bundle, begin twisting in additional fibers, either singly or in very small bundles. As the cord lengthens, the number of fibers in each strand remains roughly the same, and each strand maintains the same diameter.

Stronger, thicker cord is made by making tighter twists between your fingers. Thinner cord—as needed for fishing line—requires careful attention to ensure that new fibers are spliced into the twist only when needed to maintain a consistent diameter.

To make an even thicker, stronger cord, a third strand, produced separately, can be added to the counterclockwise twist. Alternately, the two-stranded cord can be doubled back on itself, using the same procedure to produce a four-stranded cord.

1 Twist a small bundle of fibers between thumbs and index fingers.

2 As you continue tightening the twist, it will form a kink. Secure the kink to a fixed object.

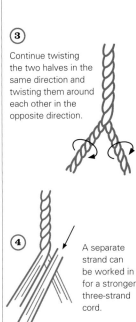

3 Continue twisting the two halves in the same direction and twisting them around each other in the opposite direction.

4 A separate strand can be worked in for a stronger three-strand cord.

TOOLS WITH YOUR KNIFE

As useful as a knife may be, there are many survival tasks it can't perform. It can, however, help you create a wide range of tools that will help you perform those tasks. We've already looked at several examples, including rabbit sticks and spears (pages 72–75), snares and traps (pages 78–85), fishing gear (pages 88–89) and fire-making tools (pages 98–107) among others. Let's look at other tools you can produce with your knife.

DIGGING STICK

Any number of wilderness activities involve digging in the ground: building a shelter, making a latrine, harvesting roots for food or cordage, digging for water, and so forth. But digging with your knife is a bad idea. At the very least, digging will quickly dull a knife, and any stones you hit may chip the edge or turn the point.

It is much better to make a digging stick from a straight hardwood branch 1.5–2" (3.5–5cm) in diameter and about 2' (60cm) long. To do this, cut a broad point at one end and a chisel point at the other, then fire-harden both ends (see page 75). You can loosen earth with the pointed end and lever out rocks with the chisel end. Scoop out loosened dirt with your hands or a flat board.

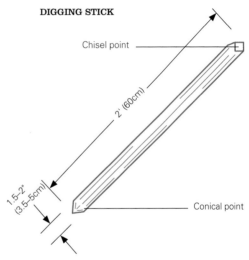

DIGGING STICK

Chisel point

2' (60cm)

1.5–2" (3.5–5cm)

Conical point

FIRE TONGS

Build a small pair of tongs for moving small hot rocks (3–4", or 7–10cm in diameter) for cooking (page 108), and a larger set for the larger rocks (6–10", or 15–25cm) you'll need to warm your bed (page 110) or expand a dugout canoe (page 147).

Cut and shape a green stick, thinning the middle as shown to serve as the hinge. Pour boiling water over the hinge while bending it slowly over a round stick. For smaller tongs, a very short piece of round stick can be inserted permanently in the hinge; this will improve both the mechanical advantage of the tongs and the longevity of the hinge. Tie a cord between the two arms to keep them at a convenient open distance.

Small rocks can be lifted with the ends of the tongs. For larger stones, you'll have better leverage if you grab the ends of the arms and use the tongs like a nutcracker, although this will expose the hinge to the fire and shorten its life.

CLAMP

This is a useful tool for working on bone spear points, fishhooks, and other small pieces. It is easy to make.

Put a blunt point on a piece of hardwood 10–16" (25–40cm) long and 1.5" (3.8cm) in diameter, then split it lengthwise. From another piece of hardwood, carve a wedge about 2" (5cm) tall at the wide end and half the length of the first stick. Tie a circle of stout cord around the stick, leaving it loose enough to insert the workpiece at the pointed end and the wedge at the other end. Depending on the work at hand, you can hold the clamp in one hand while you work with the other, or you can hold it against a log or large stone with your foot, leaving both hands free for the work.

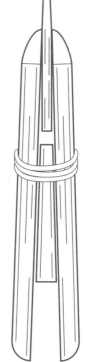

This clamp is useful for working small pieces like spear heads. Push the wedge in further for a tighter grip.

Tongs. Thin the stick in the middle to make a hinge, and tie the two sides so that you can manipulate the tool one-handed.

STONE HAMMER OR AXE

An unhafted stone often suffices as a hammer or axe. Where a handle is required, the configuration can vary according to the materials at hand.

Other than the head, there is little difference between hammers and axes. The head of a hammer can be heavier, and made of any stone that is sufficiently hard and not prone to splitting or fracturing.

Axe heads, on the other hand, are best made from rocks that can be easily split or fractured—like obsidian, flint, or slate—because these produce sharp edges. However, don't expect a stone axe to cut like a steel one, as the heads are easily broken. Cutting with a stone axe is more like vigorous shaving, with cuts made very shallow and oblique to the surface. Many tribespeople will burn a surface first, then use the axe to chop away the charred wood.

A crooked stick makes a good handle for a stone-headed adze.

STONE ADZE

An adze is essentially an axe with the head turned at a right angle. Used to hollow surfaces, not chop through them, it is the ideal tool for making wooden bowls and dugout canoes. (Wooden bowls, by the way, make durable cooking vessels for stone boiling—see page 120.) A handle with an extension that projects at an acute angle from the main shaft is useful for bracing the head. Sections of deer antler can serve the purpose well.

BOW DRILL

If equipped with a new spindle with a stone or bone point, the fire drill (see page 106) becomes a hole drill. See page 74 for advice on making spear points and page 66 for a reminder on how to notch the end of a stick. Put the two together and use the bow to spin the spindle-come-drillbit, applying downward pressure with the hand socket. A stone point does not lift the cuttings out of the hole like a modern steel twist drill, so it is necessary to stop often to clear them by hand.

A stone hammer.

WATERCRAFT

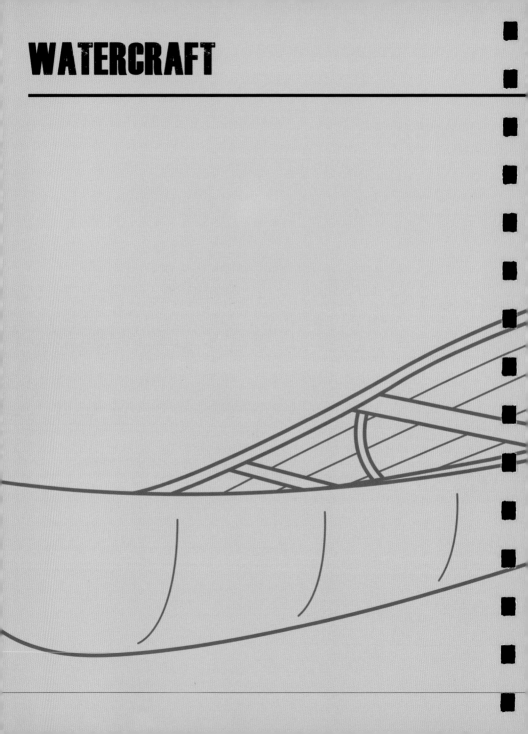

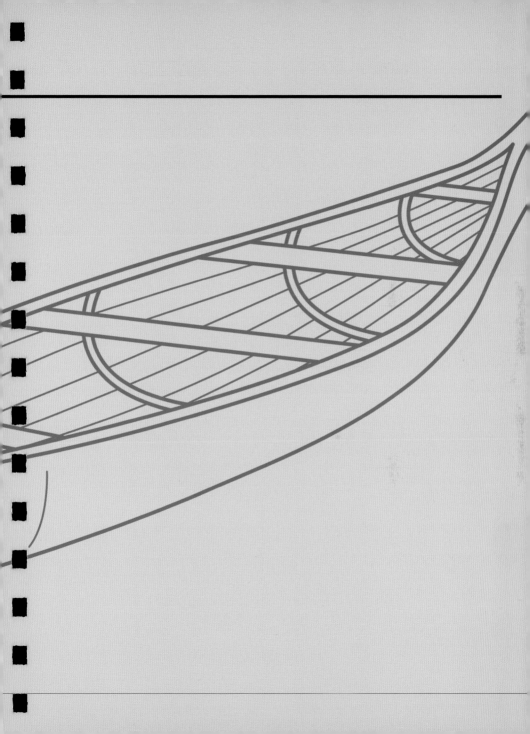

OPTIONS FOR BOATBUILDING

If rescue is not forthcoming and survival depends upon making your own way back to civilization, water may present an obstacle. It may be just a river or strait to cross, or it could be a huge lake or bay that would otherwise take weeks to hike around. But with your knife and some of the tools that you can make with a knife (see page 129), you can build a variety of boats to get you across or downstream.

HOW TO FLOAT

Watercraft float according to two different principles:

Inherent Buoyancy

Some materials are inherently buoyant and will float on their own. Rafts, for example, float because the logs from which they are assembled are less dense than water. The greatest liability of a raft is that it raises its occupants only a few inches above the water, providing little protection to people and cargo. Rafts are also generally difficult to maneuver.

TIP
Any of these boats has the potential to drown you quite dead. The suggestions here are desperate measures for desperate situations and are by no means guaranteed to ensure your safety or survival.

Floats are bundles of buoyant materials like reeds or sticks that you hang onto rather than sit or stand on—they are essentially swimming aids.

Displacement

True boats are hollow vessels that enclose air. Although they may be made from buoyant materials, they need not be. It is the displacement of water by an equal volume of comparatively lightweight air that causes a boat to float, which is why they can be made from steel or—of more interest to us—animal skins or tree bark.

PART OF A TRADITION

Some of the greatest stories of survival—both fictional and historic—involve small boats: Bligh's 1789 voyage to Timor following the *Bounty* mutiny; Shackleton's escape from Elephant Island in 1916. For our purposes, the most significant were those of Capt. Joshua Slocum who, shipwrecked in Brazil, built the junk-rigged *Liberdade* and sailed it to Boston in 1888–89, and the all-time star of survival boatbuilding, Odysseus, who, with help from the nymph Calypso, built a boat to escape from the island of Ogygia.

TYPE OF CRAFT	Pros	Cons
Float of Reeds, Sticks, or Bark	Materials abundant, easy to gather and prepare Easy to assemble Light and easy to transport	A swimming aid only; does not protect the user from the water Usefulness is time-limited, as most materials waterlog quickly
Log Raft	Materials abundant in forest environments Construction is straightforward Unsinkable for a long time	Protection from the water is limited Materials are difficult to gather Heavy: virtually impossible to transport on land Limited maneuverability
Reed Raft	Materials abundant, easy to gather and prepare Can have good maneuverability Moderately good resistance to waterlogging	Construction is time-consuming Requires a large amount of cordage Heavy: difficult to transport on land
Coracle	Quickly assembled Highly maneuverable Lightweight: excellent transportability on land Good protection from the water	Covering material may be difficult to obtain May be easily damaged Limited in navigability Limited capacity Subject to swamping
Dugout Canoe	Materials abundant in forest environments Excellent navigability Excellent protection from the water Good to excellent capacity	Materials are difficult to gather Time-consuming to build May be heavy and difficult to transport on land Subject to swamping (but maintains limited buoyancy) Damage is difficult to repair
Bark Canoe	Excellent navigability Excellent maneuverability Excellent protection from the water Excellent capacity Lightweight: excellent transportability on land Damage is easily repaired	Some materials may be difficult to obtain Very difficult and time-consuming to build Somewhat delicate Subject to swamping

FLOATS AND RAFTS

Undoubtedly the first types of watercraft used by humans, floats and rafts offer an easy way to cross a stream or other narrow body of water—as long as the water is not cold enough to kill you. Rafts can also provide long-distance transportation down a river, if you know that you will not encounter rapids, rocks, or shallows that you cannot lift the raft over.

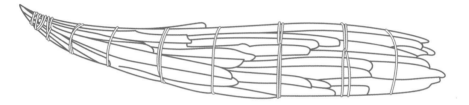

BUNDLE FLOATS

A bundle of reeds, sticks, or bark may help you over a narrow body of water with perhaps enough excess buoyancy to allow you to carry a small amount of gear on your back. Don't skimp on materials—make your bundle as big as you can handle, and test it thoroughly to ensure that it will retain its buoyancy long enough for you to complete your crossing. If there is any doubt, build a test bundle and submerge it in water near the shore, holding it down with rocks. After an hour, remove the rocks and see how well it still floats.

Remember that your forward motion will be quite slow. Holding onto the bundle with both arms, you will have only your legs for propulsion.

A long, narrow bundle is easier to propel than a round one. If making the bundle from sticks, straight ones will bundle more neatly and compactly than twisted or branching sticks.

TIP
Pre-industrial cultures have used other materials as "floats" to provide buoyancy while crossing water, including inflated skins or bladders, clay pots, and, of course, logs.

LOG RAFT

Those building a log raft face two major challenges: felling the trees and transporting them (or the assembled raft) to the water.

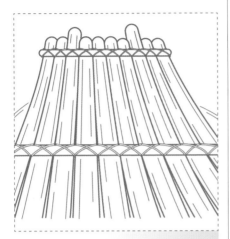

Simple in theory, rafts are not easy to build because trees are difficult to fell and transport.

Materials

You will need a minimum of three logs at least 10" (25cm) in diameter and 8–10' (2.5–3m) long, and possibly twice that volume of wood. This is a tall order if you do not have a steel axe, but fire may be used to fell the trees.

If possible, select trees with low-density wood like cottonwood (poplar). A foot or two (30–60cm) above the base of the tree, smear the bark with a thick coating of clay or mud. Build a fire at the base of the tree, all around it if you do not care which direction it falls; on one side only to fell it in that direction. (See pages 64-65 for advice on felling trees.) Keep the flames low and keep banking the coals against the tree. If the mud coating falls away, replace it to prevent the rest of the tree from burning. When the surface of the tree is well charred, remove the fire and chop away the charred material with a stone axe. Then continue the burning.

Also required are two or more very stout poles to span the logs, and a great deal of heavy cordage. If you do not have hundreds of feet of climbing rope, make the strongest cordage possible with available materials (see page 127).

Construction

Use short sections of log as rollers to transport the logs to the water's edge. Obviously, the closer to the water you fell the trees, the easier life will be. Two or more workers will have an easier time if some tow the log with ropes while the others push. When rolling a log downhill, take care to avoid being run over should the log go out of control. Once three or more logs are fastened together, the raft will be extremely difficult to move, so assemble the raft with the logs afloat if possible.

If building on solid ground, the logs must be raised several inches so that ropes can be passed beneath them. Using rollers for this purpose will also help in the raft's launching. Make the rollers at least as wide as the raft.

Place the stout poles across the logs and lash them firmly. When the raft is afloat, the logs will "work" against each other and this will put great strain on the lashings,

REED BOAT

Descendants of the Inca people in Bolivia and Peru still make reed boats on Lake Titicaca. They use tortora reeds, but bulrushes and other reeds common to North America will also work. (Thor Heyerdahl crossed the Atlantic on a raft made of papyrus—the same reeds that ancient Egyptians used to make paper.)

While straightforward in theory, a reed boat is difficult to build and requires hundreds of yards of cordage. Most consist of at least two main hulls or pontoons, built separately and then bound together. The secret to success is binding the reeds so tightly that the amount of surface exposed to water is minimized, thus slowing the process of waterlogging. The ropes encircle each reed bundle in a spiral from one end to the other. After the rope is drawn as tightly as possible, one begins again at the beginning, drawing it even tighter and taking up every fraction of an inch of slack.

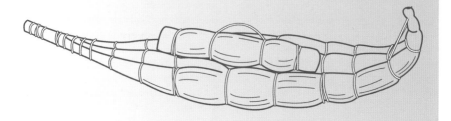

so make them as secure and numerous as possible. The working of the logs will also pose a danger to your feet or hands, but the addition of a light deck of small, straight sticks will make it safer and more comfortable.

Rafts need not be rectangular. A triangle shape can be propelled somewhat more easily, although fitting the logs together neatly may require additional woodworking.

TIP

If you'll spend a lot of time on your raft, cover a few square feet of the deck with a thick layer of mud or clay and you'll be able to cook on it.

WINTER TRAVEL

Wilderness travel in winter is difficult and dangerous and should be undertaken only in cases of absolute necessity. If possible, hunker down in camp instead, and work to stay warm and make yourself visible to rescuers. If you must travel through a frozen environment, use your knife to build tools that will make traveling easier and safer.

SNOW SHOES

Snowshoes make traveling in loose, deep snow much easier. In addition to your knife and a few sticks, you will need several yards of cordage. Leather thong is great, but nylon cord also works well.

Cut eight or ten fairly straight sticks about as tall as you are and ½–¾" (1.2–2cm) in diameter, and four more the same thickness and 6–7" (15–18cm) long. Tie the narrower ends of four or five of them together for the first shoe. If they have any curve to them, align them so that they all curve up at the lashing. Find the balance point of the bundle and tie one of the shorter pieces across the sticks, spacing them evenly. Place the ball of your foot on the crosspiece, with the toe facing toward the lashed ends, and note where your heel falls. Tie a second crosspiece under your heel.

The toe of the snowshoe must be higher than the foot platform. If the front is not already curved up, bend it up and tie it in place. After making the second shoe, tie your boots to the front crosspieces, leaving the heels loose so that they lift in a fairly natural walking motion. Cut yourself a pair of walking sticks and off you go!

KNIVES AS ICE SPIKES

Crossing a frozen lake or river on foot can be extremely hazardous. Even lakes that are solidly frozen several feet thick may have dangerously thin sections that are impossible to distinguish. If you must cross ice, equip yourself with a pair of ice stakes by fastening two rugged sheath knives together with long lanyards. (Do not use folding knives for this purpose.) Pass the lanyard through both sleeves of your coat before you put it on, and walk with both knives unsheathed in your gloved hands, points facing down. Should you break through, use the knives to stab into and drag yourself up onto solid ice.

Lanyard passes through both sleeves and connects the two knives.

SKIN BOATS

Some ethnologists believe that the skin boat—a wooden framework covered by animal hides—was mankind's first displacement craft. This seems plausible, because skin boats are easy to build compared to dugout and bark canoes, requiring little in the way of tools beside a knife for producing the light framework and an awl for sewing the hides.

to your thumb. Using your knife, remove every protrusion and rough edge. It is helpful to "sand" the sticks against a rock to smooth the surface. Carve a dozen or more "toggles," smooth chunks of wood about 3" (8cm) long and 1" (2.5cm) in diameter. Gather cordage or other binding material and a strong waterproof tarp.

CORACLE

The simplest of all skins boats is the coracle—known to American Indians as a bull boat. Roughly round in plan, they are usually small, with a capacity of just one or two people, and very light. If traveling a long distance overland, you can carry a coracle on your back with no great difficulty.

Materials

Gather a bundle of long, straight flexible sticks, ranging in thickness from your pinky finger

TIP

Since we discourage big-game hunting as a survival skill, we do not provide guidance on the preparation and sewing of animal hides for a boat covering. The construction of this coracle depends upon the availability of a rugged waterproof tarp.

Building the Framework

Using a green stick the thickness of your thumb, form a hoop 4' (1.2m) or greater in diameter. This is the gunwale—the boat's outer, upper rim. If necessary, two or more sticks can be pieced together, twisting their ends around one another and lashing them with split root. Here and elsewhere in the coracle, it is important that all lashing knots and sharp ends face the inside of the boat to protect the skin.

CORACLE FRAME
STEP 1

N

4 not visible

1 not visible

16—24"
(40–60cm)

W

3

2

1

E

2

3

4

4

3

2

1

S

4' (120cm)

Lay the hoop flat and, using a sharp stick, bore 16 holes into the ground just inside it, at least 6" (15cm) deep. Make the holes in four groups of four with 6" between the holes in each group, and the groups centered at the four "corners" of the circle. (Hereafter, the groups are referred to as "north," "south," "east," and "west," and the holes in each group are numbered 1–4 moving clockwise.) Insert a stick in the #2 hole in the north group, then bend it over and insert the other end in the corresponding #3 hole on the south side. Repeat with the #3 hole on the north, matching it with the #2 hole on the south. The height of these first arches ("frames") should be one third to one half the diameter of the hoop. Trim the arches shorter as needed.

Repeat the process with the #2 and #3 holes on the east and west sides, weaving them through the first pair of arches over-and-under. Now do the same with the #1 and #4 holes in both directions, cutting them

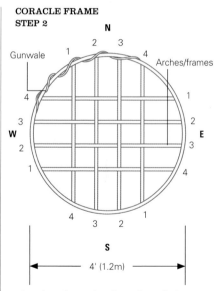

CORACLE FRAME
STEP 2

N

2   3

Gunwale

1

4

Arches/frames

4

1

3

2

W

E

2

3

1

4

4

3

2

1

S

4' (1.2m)

to length and weaving them through the other arches.

The more sticks you weave into the frame, the better it will support the skin and the less prone it will be to puncture. Make more holes in the ground between the groups of holes and add more frames. You can also add lighter-weight frames between the original eight, reducing the spacing between frames from 6" (15cm) to 3" (8cm). You need not bore holes in the ground for these extra supports: their ends need only come flush to the ground.

Pull the framework out of the ground and turn it over. Make another smaller hoop and lash it firmly to the inside of the frames, about 6" (15cm) below the gunwale. This is the "riser." Trim the ends of the frames flush with the top of the outwale and make them perfectly smooth. Now you may either form yet another hoop just inside the tops of the frames, (the "inwale") and lash the inwale, frames and outwale in place like a sandwich, or dispense with the inwale and lash the frames directly to the outwale.

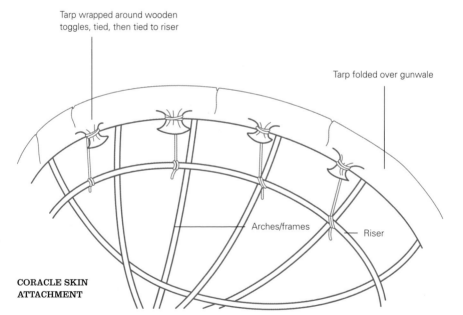

Tarp wrapped around wooden toggles, tied, then tied to riser

Tarp folded over gunwale

Arches/frames

Riser

CORACLE SKIN ATTACHMENT

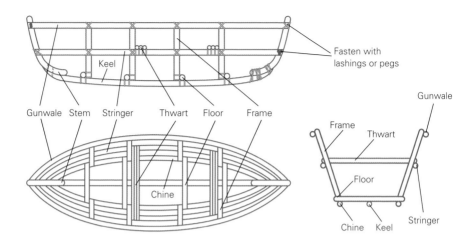

Side view, plan view, and transverse section of an umiak frame.

Skinning the Boat

Lay the tarp on the ground and fold one end over about 4" (10cm). Place toggles inside the fold, about 6" (15cm) apart. Grab a toggle through the tarp and tie a length of cord around it to hold the toggle in place, leaving several inches of "tail" hanging. Do the same with the other toggles on this edge of the tarp. Bring the edge of the tarp up and over the gunwale with the toggles on the inside, just below the gunwale. Tie the toggle cords to the riser.

Move to the opposite side of the boat, pull the tarp tight, then fasten it with toggles to the riser. If you don't want to cut the tarp, fold it as far as necessary and leave the excess hanging outside the boat for now. Work your way around, pulling the tarp tight and tying it to the riser with toggles and cords. Work to minimize wrinkles on the outside. Take any excess length of tarp and fold it into the boat, protecting the skin from the inside. If you do not have excess tarp, lay bunches of grass in the bottom to protect the skin from being punctured from inside.

OTHER SKIN BOATS

A coracle is appropriate for crossing small calm rivers or fishing on lakes, but it is slow and lacks directional stability. An umiak (or its Irish equivalent, the curragh) is seaworthy and fast, and, if a long tarp is available for the skin, a viable alternative to a bark canoe or a dugout. The frame is relatively easy to build.

DUGOUT CANOES

Dugout canoes are still in everyday use in many parts of the world for good reason: they are handy, durable, and easy (although time-consuming) to build from readily available materials. And if you doubt their seaworthiness, consider: most of the islands throughout the vast Pacific Ocean were settled by people arriving in dugout canoes, along with their families, pigs, and all the impedimenta required to begin farming.

FELLING AND SHAPING

See pages 64–65 for advice on felling and limbing trees.

A single-hull dugout canoe requires a tree at least 20" (50cm) in diameter—hard to come by in some areas. Smaller trees of 16–18" (40–45cm) or so can suffice for a double-hull canoe or one with an outrigger. The trunk must be straight and free of flaws for the entire length of the boat—figure at least 10' (3m) for one person. Although almost any tree that fits that description can be made into a canoe, a light, easily carved tree like cottonwood (poplar) has obvious advantages.

Work in the shade to prevent the hull from drying quickly and cracking. When you're not working on it, cover it with wet leaves to retard drying.

The outside is shaped first, with the boat upside down. After the tree is felled and limbed, block it or stake it in place so that it does not move. Strip the bark and draw the

TIP

A string stretched between two points helps define a straight line. By rubbing charcoal on the string first, you can use it like a mason's chalk line.

outlines on the bare wood with charcoal in plan view (i.e., from above) and profile view (from the side). Rounded ends are buoyant and relatively easy to produce. A scow-shaped bow and square stern are even easier. Narrow, hollow ends are the most efficient through the water, but require the most careful work.

Between the ends, draw straight lines to define the sides, but remember that, while you're drawing the lines along the boat's bottom, the lines must be projected mentally down to the gunwale. Hewing the sides is extremely difficult without a steel axe. If you lack one, leave the sides as they are.

Work the ends with your knife or stone axe, constantly sighting them from above and from both sides. Redraw the lines as needed.

SHAPING THE INTERIOR

Roll the hull over and reblock it to keep it in place. Looking at the log from the side, draw in the boat's sheerline from one end to the other. A straight sheerline is easiest to make, but, as we will see, there are advantages to cutting a reverse sheer, making the edges rise toward the middle.

Using your knife, axe, or adze, make a flat surface 6–8" (15–20cm) wide all along the length of the trunk. Build a low fire along the length of this platform except at the very ends, or build a fire nearby and transfer hot coals onto it. Allow the surface to char several inches deep, then remove the fire, allow the wood to cool, and chop or

scrape away the char with an axe, adze, sharp rock, or shells. Repeat the process until you approach the sheerline. Apply mud or clay to the sheerline to protect it from burning, then proceed as before, working your way slowly down into the trunk.

In the New World dugout canoes were constructed by a process of burning and scraping.

Another way to monitor the thickness of the sides of the hull as you carve is to make a set of fixed calipers. Although it is possible to do the same for the bottom, the calipers would be large and awkward. An easier approach is to fasten straight sticks horizontally across the sheer and against the outer bottom, then use a length of stick or string to compare the distance between the sticks with the distance between the upper stick and the bottom of the boat in its interior.

Bottom depth gauge

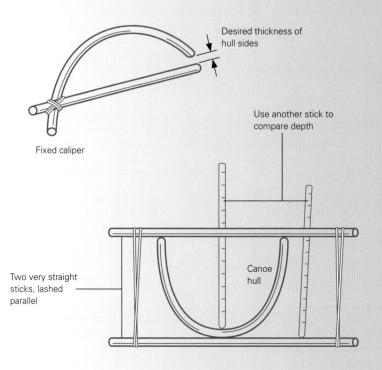

Desired thickness of hull sides

Use another stick to compare depth

Fixed caliper

Two very straight sticks, lashed parallel

Canoe hull

EXPANDING THE HULL

Most dugout canoes are very narrow and very round, and this makes them very unstable. Both stability and capacity can be improved by expanding, or widening, the hull.

Fill the hull with water, and heat a large number of rocks as big as you can handle. Using tongs (page 130), transfer the rocks into the water. If you can make the whole canoe boil, you're doing well. As the rocks give up their heat, replace them with more hot rocks.

Keep it up until the sides of the canoe become flexible enough to bend outward using stout sticks that are just a little bit longer than the canoe's inside width.

As the canoe bends out in the middle, the sheer will depress and the ends will rise. If you began with a reverse sheer (see above), the end result may be either a straight sheer or a traditionally-shaped concave one.

MORE HULLS FOR YOUR DUGOUT

Turning a dugout canoe into a multi-hull craft increases its stability and its carrying capacity more than is possible by expanding the hull. Aside from the additional labor, an important downside is that the canoe becomes fairly worthless for use on narrow, twisting streams.

An outrigger can be easily contrived by fastening outrigger poles across the gunwales, first boring holes just below the sheerline as lashing points. Choose poles that curve downward so that the outrigger float just kisses the water. The float itself should

be made from the lightest wood possible, and tapered at both ends. Build a light platform of sticks between the poles for carrying cargo.

Double canoes can be lashed side by side, exactly doubling the carrying capacity and the amount of work. For even greater capacity and stability, the hulls can be spaced further apart, but this requires an extremely rugged framework to resist the severe torquing forces that will attempt to separate them. A large cargo platform can be carried on the framework between the hulls.

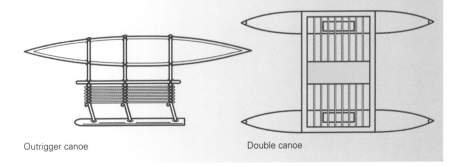

Outrigger canoe   Double canoe

BARK CANOES

The birchbark canoe of the North American Indian is one of the finest boat types ever created by an indigenous people. Light and strong, they could negotiate narrow, twisty streams, navigate on the ocean, and carry hundreds of pounds of cargo—all in a package that could be carried by one man and built and repaired with materials readily available in the environment.

MATERIALS

Gathering materials for a bark canoe is a major part of the process. Get started on this long before you expect to begin construction proper.

Bark

The best bark for canoes comes from the white or paper birch. It is flexible, elastic, waterproof, and relatively easy to remove from the tree in large sections. In its absence, several other trees may be utilized, including spruce, fir, white pine, elm, and eucalyptus. If you can find a tree with a smooth, perfect bark, free of branches over the length of the canoe and wide enough to extend from gunwale to gunwale in a single piece, you will save much time and effort in the boat's construction. Should the ideal tree not present itself, you will have to make do by piecing together smaller pieces of bark.

Depending upon the species and the time of year, the bark may come off easily or with much difficulty. Your objective is to remove it with as few cracks and tears as possible. Make a vertical cut down the trunk of the length required. At the top and bottom of the cut, make horizontal cuts entirely around the tree. Use wedges to loosen the bark from the trunk along the whole length of the vertical cut and peel it back bit by bit. Don't allow it to fall to the ground all at once—it will crack. If necessary, tie it loosely to the tree before it has entirely separated from the trunk, and ease it down slowly.

Birch bark should be used immediately or soaked to keep it moist and flexible. Keep all bark moist during construction.

Woodwork

The traditional North American birchbark canoe requires a fair amount of woodwork: wood gunwales form the main structural member; thin slats of wood laid lengthwise sheath the entire interior surface of the bark to stiffen it; the sheathing is held in place by closely spaced bent ribs that curve from one gunwale down into the bottom and up to the opposite gunwale. White cedar is ideal for all of these: it is easily split and easy

TIP

A traditional Indian-style canoe takes a long time to construct. The version described here is simplified to expedite construction. It will not be as capable—and certainly not as lovely—as a traditional birchbark canoe.

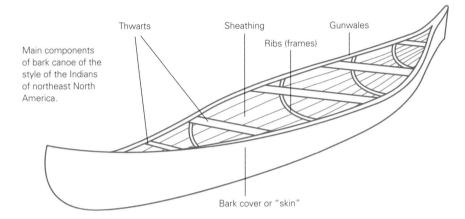

Main components of bark canoe of the style of the Indians of northeast North America.

Thwarts · Sheathing · Gunwales · Ribs (frames) · Bark cover or "skin"

to bend and work. Thwarts—cross-pieces between the gunwales—may be of any wood.

The woodwork for your canoe may be considerably less in amount and complexity. Birch bark, being quite flexible, requires a fair amount of internal stiffening, but canoes built of other barks may get by with less. The Yamana people of Tierra del Fuego used no sheathing and only a light structure of a few widely spaced frames, thwarts, and gunwales. Certain Australian bark canoes had no ribs, sheathing, or gunwales—only a couple of sticks to hold their sides apart. These were used only in swamps and other completely calm conditions, however. Assess your needs and build the simplest boat that will satisfy them.

Lashings

See the sidebar on page 128 for information on harvesting spruce roots, which are the traditional material for lashing canoe parts together. After harvesting, roll them into a tight circle and soak them in water for a few days, then scrape off the bark. Using your thumbnail, split them lengthwise at least in half, and then into quarters if necessary to achieve a maximum width of $\frac{3}{16}$" (5mm). You will need a few dozen yards in all.

Other tying materials may be used as long as they retain their strength when wet. Rawhide thongs will work if they are allowed to dry out between use to prevent rot.

Sealant

Seams between sections of bark must be sealed with a waterproofing sealant. Pine sap, the traditional choice, is easy but time-consuming to collect. Some may be scraped from the bark of trees with a twig, but this will yield only small quantities. To encourage its flow, slash the bark of several trees deeply in several places. Gather it in a metal container, if available, for it must be heated when applied. (See below.)

A far less appealing but possibly more expedient sealant is clay or mud, as used by Australian natives in some of their bark canoes. Although considerably less waterproof and flexible than pine sap, it is ubiquitous and easily replaced when needed. If you will always remain within easy reach of shore, mud may suffice.

CONSTRUCTION

The following procedures are a combination of North American and Australian bark canoe building methods, with other expedients mixed in to make construction as quick and simple as possible. Bear in mind that your canoe, intended for a one-time voyage of survival, and perhaps built with non-traditional materials, might dispense with certain components and procedures that would otherwise be deemed essential in a canoe intended for long-term use in a wider range of conditions.

Gunwales

Construction begins with the gunwales, which, when assembled, also serve as a building form.

- Get out a pair of poles a little longer than the canoe and at least 1½" (4cm) in diameter.
- Carve a center thwart about 30" (76cm).

- Lash the gunwales together tightly at one end.
- Lash the thwart to the midpoints of the gunwales.
- Pull the gunwales together at the opposite end and lash them.
- For canoes over 12' (4m), add an additional thwart halfway between the middle thwart and each end.

Shape the Bark

- Lay the bark flat with its outer surface facing up. Bark with a thick, stiff outer rind (most species except birch) must be scraped smooth.
- Lay the building form on the bark and weight it down with stones.
- Bend the bark up along the sides of the building form.
- Drive stakes into the ground just outside the folded-up bark sides.
- Where the bark sides do not follow the curve of the building form and buckle outward, heat (do not burn) the bark with fire or pour boiling water on it and fold in the excess.
- Use split sticks to clamp the folds, or bore a few holes straight through all three layers

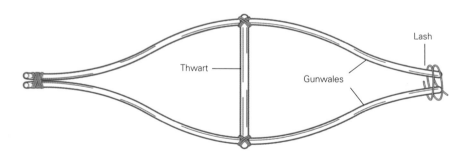

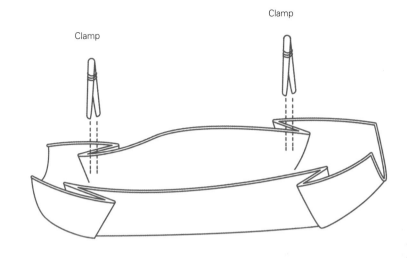

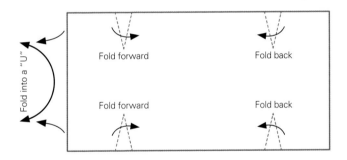

near the top edge and tie them together with lengths of split spruce root.

- If the bark will not fold flat, use your knife to cut out long, narrow triangles, with the narrow base at the upper edge of the bark, and sew the edges together as described in the next procedure.

Extend the Sides

The sides should be a minimum 8" (20cm), and preferably 11–12" (28–30cm) tall amidships. If they are not high enough:

- Offset the building form and refold the bark so that it is tall enough on one side. This will reduce the number of seams you have to sew.
- Cut a strip of bark to make up the shortage on one side, allowing at least 1" (2.5cm) overlap.
- Holding the patch in position, bore holes with an awl through both layers of bark and stitch them together with split

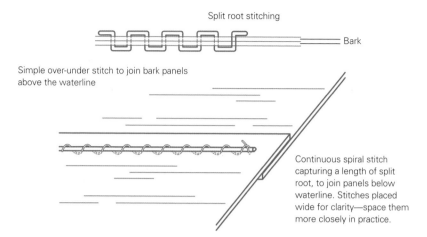

Split root stitching

Bark

Simple over-under stitch to join bark panels above the waterline

Continuous spiral stitch capturing a length of split root, to join panels below waterline. Stitches placed wide for clarity—space them more closely in practice.

spruce root. If the seam will be above the waterline, a simple over-under-over stitch through a single row of holes will suffice.

- Seams below the waterline require 2" (5cm) of overlap. Bore a double row of holes ¾" (1.9cm) apart and use a continuous spiral stitch, locking a section of half-round split root under the stitches on the exterior of the bark.
- If you are not using pine sap as a seam sealant, smear a thick layer of wet clay on the mating surfaces of the bark before sewing them together. Pine sap sealant may be applied later.

Attach the Gunwales, Enclose the Ends

- Remove the stones and raise the gunwale assembly to its proper height, supporting it from below or clamping or tying it to the stakes.
- Trim the top edge of the bark flush with the top of the gunwale.
- Bore holes in the bark just below the gunwale and lash the two together with a simple spiral wrap. When you reach the end

of a section of root, a single overhand knot against the gunwale will usually suffice to hold it in place. Begin lashing with the next piece of root in the next hole. Lash up both sides along their entire length.

- Crease the bark of the ends together, using heat or boiling water as needed. Trim the bow and stern profiles.
- Bore a series of holes 1" (2.5cm) back from the ends of the bark. Seal and stitch the seams as above.

Sheathing and Frames

- If there are any holes in the bark, seal them at this time. You may apply a patch on the interior using pine sap sealant. (See below for details.)
- Get out a number of long battens just a bit shorter than the canoe. These can be 2–4" (5–8cm) wide and ¼–1" (6–25mm) tall. The number required depends upon the stiffness of the bark and the degree of ruggedness desired. You might sheath the entire interior, or space them widely and use as few as five or six per side.

- If you can't get pieces long enough for the battens, put a long taper on the ends of shorter pieces so they lie neatly against each other, end-over-end, to the length required.
- Lay the battens inside the hull.
- Cut flexible sticks of various lengths and bend them into a U-shape inside the hull, forcing their tops against the underside of the gunwales so that they hold the battens in place against the bark. These are temporary clamps, used only while you make and install proper frames.
- Get out a number of flat frames in various lengths. Cedar is best, but ash, pine, and other flexible woods will work. Pour boiling water on one of the longest, for use in the middle of the canoe. Using your knee, bend two rounded "corners" into it, forming a shallow U-shape. Tie a cord around its circumference to hold it in shape while it cooks and dries.
- Place the upper ends of the frame beneath the gunwales amidships, with the bottom of the frame angled aft. Using a blunt stick and a mallet, drive the bottom of the frame forward so that it slides over the battens, until the frame lies in a vertical plane. The bark will stretch a bit, and the tops of the frame will be locked in against the bottom of the gunwales by the bark's tension.
- If hammering the frame into place takes too much effort, stop before you tear the bark. Trim the tops of the frame and try again.
- Install the rest of the frames in like manner.

- The ends of the canoe are too narrow for a bent frame. If it is necessary to stiffen the ends, cut a "headboard" from a solid plank to stretch the bark and brace up the gunwales on both sides.

Sealing Seams
- Heat a pint (500ml) of pine sap in a pan until it is a thin liquid. Skim or strain out debris through a coarse cloth.
- If you have a source of fat, melt a few spoons full into the sap.
- Mix in a little wood ash or finely ground charcoal.
- While it is still liquid, brush the sap mixture into all bark seams. Fill all stitching holes and any pinholes in the bark.

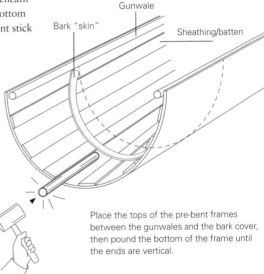

Gunwale

Bark "skin"

Sheathing/batten

Place the tops of the pre-bent frames between the gunwales and the bark cover, then pound the bottom of the frame until the ends are vertical.

BOAT PROPULSION

In the evening, when you're relaxing around the fire after a hard day of boatbuilding, take out your knife and start work on your means of propulsion, be it a pole, a paddle, or a sailing rig. Depending upon the boat and the conditions you anticipate, you might want all three.

CANOE POLE

Almost as easy to make as it is to describe, a pole is a surprisingly effective way to propel a canoe. Unlike a paddle, you can use it to move upstream against a fairly swift current. Moving downstream, you can "snub" yourself against the bottom, stopping dead and picking your way carefully, foot by foot, through a rock garden. In water that's too deep to reach bottom, a pole is a surprisingly effective substitute for a double-bladed paddle, making it a perfectly reasonable way to cross lakes.

Cut the straightest hardwood stick you can find, 1.5–2" (3.8–5cm) in diameter at the butt and 12–13' (3.5–4m) long. Trim off every hint of a knot and sand it with a piece of sandstone until it slides through your hands like silk.

PADDLES

The coracle is paddled over the "front"—in other words, whichever way you're facing in this round boat. Since you're sitting very low, the paddle should have a very short shaft. The blade should be wide.

Canoes are generally propelled with a single-bladed paddle, but inexperienced canoeists often find it easier to make a canoe go where they want with a double-bladed paddle. Many also find the double-bladed paddle less strenuous to use.

The shape of the paddle blade is not terribly important, but on a single-bladed paddle, the shape of the shaft is. Make it gently oval, with the long axis perpendicular to the blade faces. A widened grip on the end of the shaft is essential for good control.

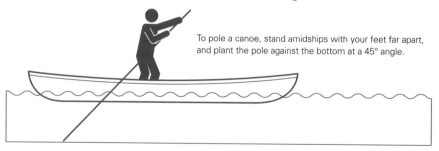

To pole a canoe, stand amidships with your feet far apart, and plant the pole against the bottom at a 45° angle.

TYPES OF SAIL RIGS

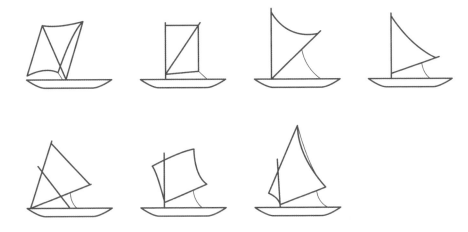

Effective sails can be made in a variety of shapes. All of these rigs are capable of upwind sailing.

SAIL RIGS

With the exception of the coracle, all the boats discussed here can be sailed downwind with a simple squaresail rig consisting of two poles or spars: a vertical mast, and a horizontal yard from which the sail hangs. Steering can be done with a paddle over the stern, and the sail can be made from a tarp, a blanket, a sheet of plastic, or woven matting (see pages 123–124). Neither spar need be especially straight and, in the interests of safety, the rig should be kept small. In order to avoid capsizing, any sail rig in a narrow monohull canoe must be capable of being "struck" (i.e., taken down) at a moment's notice should the wind change direction.

Only the outrigger and double canoes can sail against the wind without the addition of centerboards or leeboards. The range of rig styles capable of upwind sailing is enormous.

AXES

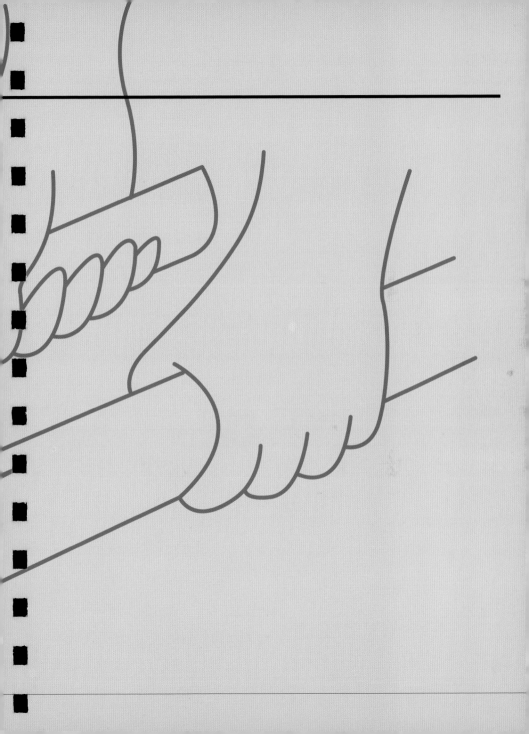

HATCHETS AND AXES

All outdoor travelers should, carry knives. But while knives are versatile, they are not the ideal tools for all situations. Many of the tasks we've discussed are difficult to perform with a knife, and we have covered them on the assumption that, in a survival situation, you will be willing to perform difficult work. Nonetheless, some tasks are more easily performed with an axe and, because many who travel through wilderness woodlands carry axes, it makes sense to turn to them as useful survival tools.

A NOTE ABOUT TERMINOLOGY

Let's get a bit of nomenclature out of the way first. *Hatchet* (also: *hand axe*) means a one-handed axe, while *axe* is the general term covering both the one-handed and two-handed versions. These distinctions are generally, if not quite universally, accepted, and that's how we'll use them in this book. *Tomahawks* are small hatchets intended for use as weapons, and are not addressed here.

TYPES OF AXES

When browsing among axe choices, you'll find three sizes, corresponding to three basic types.

Hatchet

Backpackers and others who travel light rarely carry any axe larger than a hatchet. The handle or haft is usually about 12" (30cm) long, and the weight is usually around 1 pound (0.5kg). Anything more is simply too much to carry. Hatchets are intended for processing kindling and splitting only very small logs for firewood, but they can be pressed into service on bigger tasks when required.

Camp Axe

With a handle about 24" (60cm) long and a weight of about 2 pounds (1kg), the camp axe is the smallest two-handed axe. Much better for splitting firewood than a hatchet, it is a favorite among canoeists and horse trekkers, who can carry more kit than backpackers.

General-Purpose Axe

Most full-size axes weigh between 4 and 6 pounds (2–3kg) and have handles 28–36" (71–91cm) long. Greater mass and leverage makes a full-size, general-purpose axe by far the best choice if you want to fell and

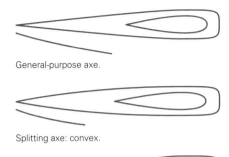

General-purpose axe.

Splitting axe: convex.

Limbing axe: concave.

limb a tree and split big firewood. Perhaps surprisingly, it is also the safest design.

HEAD SHAPE

Less obvious than overall size, the cross-sectional shape of an axe's head also affects its performance. A narrow, concave head can take the sharpest edge; this type is especially good for limbing, which requires cutting across the grain of the wood. Strongly convex blades are best for splitting logs into firewood, their broad wedge shape working to separate the fibers lengthwise rather than cut through them. The best axe for general-purpose use is a compromise between these: slightly convex for effective splitting, yet thin enough for limbing.

DOUBLE-BITTED AXES

Axes with two blades do not make good survival tools. Heavy and dangerous, they were invented for professional loggers whose productivity was measured in the number of trees felled per day. By sharpening two blades at once, they could cut twice as much before having to stop to resharpen.

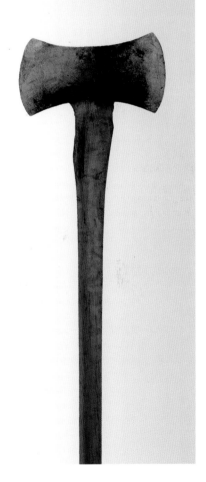

CARRYING AND STORING AXES

A surprising number of axe injuries occur when the axe isn't even in use: they occur when the axe is being carried, or when its entirely at rest but "stored" in such a way as to present a danger to those around it. If you're going to get hurt, at least do it while you're working, okay?

SHEATHS

Every axe should be equipped with a sheath. If yours doesn't have one, don't take it anywhere except to the hardware store to get one that fits properly. Just by virtue of its mass, a sharp axe is bound to cut things unless its edge is protected, so the sheath must be used whenever the axe is in transit, whether you are carrying it or have it packed with your gear.

Sheaths for hatchets often have belt loops, but most people find it awkward to carry a hatchet at their waist, unless it has a particularly short handle, no more than 8" (20cm).

IN THE PACK

It's rare that you would need a hatchet at a moment's notice in any case (unlike a knife), so you might as well pack it with your gear. If you are backpacking, place it as low as possible, along with other heavy gear, to maintain the lowest center of gravity.

Larger axes must be lashed to the outside of the pack. The head should be at the bottom for the best balance.

CARRYING UNSHEATHED

Although we just warned you to never carry an axe unsheathed, it is really inevitable that you will carry a bare axe on occasion, if only for short distances. Make sure you do it safely. Carry the axe by the handle just below the head with the edge facing down or to the outside. Don't carry it over your shoulder: one stumble, and you could lose an ear. If you do trip with a bare axe in your hand, get rid of it! Before you stick out your hands to break your fall, throw the axe to the side to make sure you don't land on it. For this reason, don't let anyone walk on that side of you when you're carrying an axe.

CAMP STORAGE

In camp, an axe gets so much use that it often does not make sense to replace the sheath every time. If there's more than one person using the axe, a constantly replaced sheath will almost certainly get lost. If your axe will be left out for general use during the day, stash the sheath where you can find it, and show your traveling partners where and how they should leave the axe.

TIP
Treat leather sheaths with neatsfoot oil or other leather protectant. The oil will inhibit rust on the axe head.

Safe: hold the axe just below the head, with the edge facing out.

Unsafe: over your shoulder

Here are the rules:

- If it's sharp enough to cut wood, it's sharp enough to cut through a boot, so never leave an axe lying on the ground.
- Driving the head into a standing tree is another bad idea. With the handle sticking out, it risks being bumped loose, in which case it could fall onto someone's head, shoulder, or foot. It's also bad for the tree.
- Leaning it against the base of a tree, with the head down, eliminates the risk of the axe falling from a height, but it will almost certainly be knocked over many times in the course of a day, and the head could still be inadvertently kicked—possibly with a bare foot.
- Driving the head into a stump is pretty good, because the handle is usually pretty

hard to miss. Still, someone could run into it. Angle the handle as close to vertical as possible to avoid this.

- Driving the head into either the end or the top surface of a fallen log, with the handle over the trunk, eliminates almost all possible accidents. You can't run into the handle unless you're drunk enough to fall over the log.

SHARPENING AXES

As with all cutting tools, a sharp axe is safer than a dull one. Dull tools require more effort to use, and if you're swinging an axe with all your might, your accuracy is sure to suffer. A dull axe is more likely to glance or bounce off its target, sending it in a direction that could be…highly inconvenient. By cutting more quickly and effectively, a sharp axe will also reduce your fatigue and enable you to perform more work.

As you stroke the file forward, extreme care must be taken to avoid contacting the edge with your "on" hand.

FILES

Badly dulled or damaged blades must be sharpened first with a "mill bastard" file—usually 8–10" (25cm) long with a single-cut pattern that cuts only on the forward stroke. Don't "saw" this file back and forth: instead, use a light pushing stroke, and lift the file on the return. Most people file away from the edge, and this is the safer approach. If you file toward the edge, wear leather work gloves and hold the file in such a way so that, if you stroke too far, you will not cut yourself.

If the edge is badly nicked, you will have to file down the edge from the top until you reach the bottom of the nick. Of course, this will eliminate the sharp edge entirely and create a large flat spot on the blade's curved profile. Don't worry about the curve: just file the edge sharp again, then move on to a medium whetstone. Numerous repeated resharpenings will reestablish the curve without any particular attention.

WHETSTONES

A round whetstone with two grades—medium-coarse on one side, and fine on the other—is a good general-purpose sharpening tool for axes, and small enough to fit into any kit. These are available as oil stones and water stones, the latter being more practical for use in the field.

Hold the whetstone around its upper edge with the tips of your fingers, taking care to keep them away from the axe blade. Starting with the coarser side, use a circular motion and gentle pressure. Stop periodically to wipe the metal particles from the surface of the stone. When you have removed the file marks with the medium side, move to the fine side of the stone and continue until you have removed the coarser stone's scratches. The effect is to produce a perfectly smooth edge, minimizing the size of the microscopic "teeth" that interfere with the blade's ability to slice through wood fibers.

To remove a nick, file the edge down flat, then resharpen.

SAFE AXE USE

Careless and ill-informed axe use can easily injure or kill users and bystanders. Beyond the obvious danger of a poorly aimed axe hitting a person directly, axes may bounce off their targets, hitting users on the rebound. Trees do not always fall in the direction expected, and falling and felled trees create further dangers that we'll discuss on pages 166–168.

USING A HATCHET

Although it has the least mass and leverage, a hatchet may be the most dangerous type of axe. Because of its short handle, the head is never far from your body, so a strike that bounces or glances off its target could end up hitting you.

Felling

When chopping a standing tree, place your feet at least 3' (1m) away from its base and lean against the trunk, supporting yourself by your off hand. By chopping the trunk no more than 12" (30cm) from the ground, any glancing stroke will deflect into the ground rather than your foot or leg.

1 Limbing

Limbs must be cut where they meet the trunk, not 1' (30cm) away from it where they will make the axe bounce. To the extent possible, position yourself on the opposite side of the trunk from the limb being cut. Hold the axe away from your body and stroke mainly from the shoulder, so that the head travels in a straight line away from you. If instead you hold your elbow close to your body and swing from the elbow, the axe head will move in an arc.

In the event of bounce-back, it could arc back and hit you in the face.

2 TWO-HANDED AXE USE

The swing of a two-handed axe requires practice. The off hand remains stationary, gripping the handle just above the butt. Place the dominant hand just above it. On the back-swing, as the head rises above your dominant-side shoulder, the dominant hand slides about three-quarters the length of the handle to within a few inches of the head. On the down stroke, the dominant hand slides back down the handle to meet the top of the off hand.

When felling a tree, place your feet at least an axe-length from its base. Bend at the waist and swing over your dominant shoulder. The stroke should angle down at about 45°. Any flatter and it will not cut effectively; any steeper and it is likely to deflect into the ground. Never cut upward, as a glancing stroke could hit you in the head.

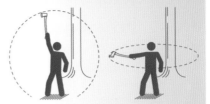

- Wear work boots, long trousers, a long-sleeve shirt, and eye protection. Hard hats, though unlikely in most survival scenarios, are considered essential safety gear when felling trees.

- Keep the edge sharp. A sharp axe is less prone to deflect than a dull one.

- Never chop anything springy. A small branch has more "bounce" 1' (30cm) away from a trunk than where the branch and trunk meet. A sapling may be too springy to chop 3' (1m) from the ground, but firm enough at a height of 12" (30cm).

- Work free of obstructions. You should be able to hold the axe at full extension and swing it in complete circles horizontally and vertically without encountering interference.

- Keep bystanders at least 10' (3m) away.

- Position your work and angle your cuts to minimize the possibility of a deflected stroke.

- Position your body out of the path of any possible deflected stroke.

FELLING

Felling—chopping a tree down—is undeniably dangerous. Even to experienced woodsmen, trees fall in unexpected ways, influenced by their species, health, shape, angle of lean, wind, surrounding trees, and other factors. But if felling doesn't kill you, it might help you survive. This is a general introduction and not a comprehensive guide. The best way to learn is under the instruction of an experienced professional.

GENERAL SAFETY

When felling trees, avoid all sources of difficulty and potential danger until you have gained experience. Specifically, avoid trees that:

- are greater than 12" (30cm) in diameter
- lean more than 2° (dead vertical is best)
- are crooked
- are located on slopes or unstable ground
- are close to boulders or crowded by other trees
- have markedly asymmetrical tops
- show signs of disease or fire damage
- have dead branches too high to limb before felling

Additionally, before you begin chopping:

- Be aware that even a light breeze will likely determine a tree's direction of fall. Never fell in high winds.
- Decide where you will escape to safety when the tree begins to fall. Identify an alternate route to safety should it fall in an unexpected direction.
- Clear escape routes by removing brush and low branches.

DETERMINING THE VERTICAL

Use your axe as a plumb to determine a tree's angle of lean. Hold the axe by the butt with the head down, at arm's length, and line it up visually with the trunk. Do this all around the tree, not just from one location.

FELLING CUTS

Two cuts are required to fell a tree safely. The first cut, known as the undercut, is made on the side to which you want the tree to fall. The backcut is made second, on the opposite side and slightly higher. The two must not meet: they purposely fall short of one another to leave a "hinge." This is essential to control the direction of the tree's fall, and to prevent the base from kicking back toward you.

Stop after the first stroke or two on the undercut, step back several paces from the tree and look up, trying to identify any loose, dead branches that might fall. The top of the undercut should be made at a 45° angle, and the bottom should be level and 12" (30cm) from the ground. Cut through only about one third of the trunk.

Make the backcut exactly opposite the undercut and about 2" (5cm) higher. The backcut does not overlap the undercut: it must stop 2" (5cm) or more before it reaches that depth. As the backcut progresses, step back after every few strokes and look at the top of the tree, trying to detect the beginning of its lean.

Make sure the hinge is perfectly level on both sides. A hinge that is cut at an angle will cause the tree to twist or slide sideways as it falls.

The moment the tree begins to move, step away quickly the full distance of the height of the tree. The safety zone is in area about 120–150° on either side from the intended direction of fall, and behind a strong tree if possible. Directly opposite the direction of fall is not particularly safe for several reasons:

- If you misjudged the wind or the tree's angle of lean (but left a good hinge), it is more likely to fall in the opposite direction to the safety zone.

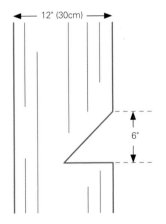

Cut the front notch or undercut first.

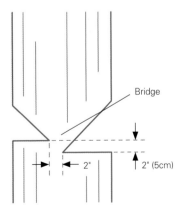

The back or felling notch is higher than the undercut. The two must not overlap.

SAFETY & DANGER ZONES

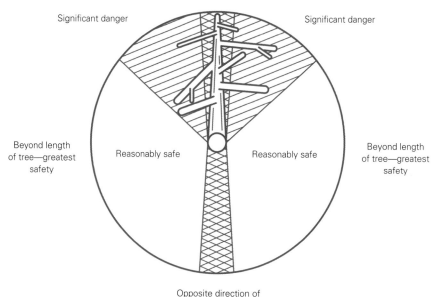

Intended direction of
fall—greatest danger

Significant danger

Significant danger

Beyond length
of tree—greatest
safety

Reasonably safe

Reasonably safe

Beyond length
of tree—greatest
safety

Opposite direction of
fall—significant danger

- The butt could kick back in the opposite direction.
- If the tree is diseased or weak and it catches another tree as it falls, the top could break off in the opposite direction.

If the tree hangs up on another tree, give it up as a bad job and stay away from it. Without considerable expertise and heavy equipment, there is no safe way to get it down. It will fall by itself eventually, and you want to be nowhere near when that happens. For this reason, it is best to fell a tree into a clearing, and to avoid trees that are crowded by others.

LIMBING AND SECTIONING

Now that the tree is down, you need to process it into usable pieces: firewood, poles for shelter, a dugout canoe, or whatever. The first step is to remove the limbs; the next is to cut the trunk and large branches into shorter sections.

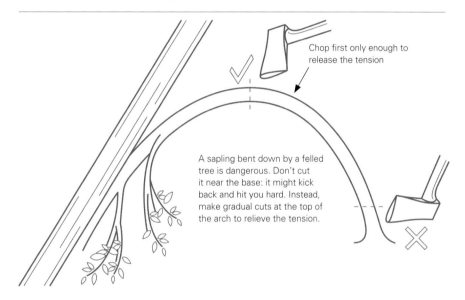

Chop first only enough to release the tension

A sapling bent down by a felled tree is dangerous. Don't cut it near the base: it might kick back and hit you hard. Instead, make gradual cuts at the top of the arch to relieve the tension.

RELEASE SOME TENSION

A sapling that has been bent down by a fallen tree is a dangerous thing. If you were to cut it at the base, the butt could spring out at you viciously. Cutting it higher up on the outside could cause an instant split with the same results. Relieve the tension by cutting the underside of the bend, staying alert for signs of collapse and remaining out of the path of spring-back when it breaks through. The same holds true for the tree's own branches that may hold the trunk off the ground.

LIMBING

Keep the trunk between the limb and your feet. Do not straddle the trunk or stand on the same side as the limb. Cut limbs in the direction they grow. On most trees, where the limbs grow upward from the trunk, this means starting at the lowest limbs and cutting them from the bottom.

Small limbs may be cut with strokes almost flush to the trunk. Larger branches are cut by removing wedge-shaped sections, first chopping perpendicular to the trunk near the limb's base, then chopping flush to the trunk to meet the first cut. Do not chop a limb any distance away from the trunk, or you risk having the axe head bounce straight back at you.

BUCKING

Logs are best cut into sections, or bucked, from the side rather than the top. Logs 6–16" (15–40cm) in diameter should be bucked from the opposite side to protect your feet and legs. Logs smaller than that should be backed up with a larger log, which you stand behind. Stand on top of logs larger than 16" (40cm) in diameter and cut below your feet.

Make the cut vertical, and chop at 45° from the surface, alternating directions from the perpendicular so that the cut opens up at an angle of 90°. To avoid having to make the cuts any wider than necessary, change sides when you are halfway through. Offset the second cut a few inches from the first so that the final stroke does not pass straight through and endanger your legs.

CUTTING THROUGH A LARGE DOWN LOG

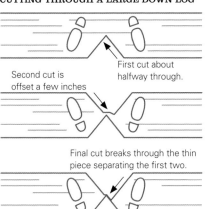

Second cut is offset a few inches

First cut about halfway through.

Final cut breaks through the thin piece separating the first two.

MEDIUM LOGS

If a downed log is too small to stand on but too large to chop against a protector log, stand facing away from it and stroke back and to your off side.

SMALL LOGS

Small logs that won't stay put by their own weight can be wedged against a protector log, which will save your feet when you break through.

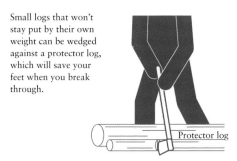

Protector log

CHOPPING BELOW YOUR FEET

Make sure the log is absolutely stable. Never aim your strokes near the top surface of the log.

SPLITTING AND HEWING

Split wood takes fire much more readily than whole logs. Given the importance of fire building in wilderness survival—and occasionally the need to build one quickly—splitting can be an essential skill. If you're staying put, split enough wood in one session to keep yourself supplied for several days.

SPLITTING FIREWOOD

In a survival situation, log sections will rarely be square-ended, as they would be if cut with a chainsaw. Therefore, a flat-topped chopping block, usually so handy when splitting firewood, will be of little use. Instead, find a solid fallen trunk with a handy crotch in which to brace your work.

Short log sections may be stood upright in the crotch and split from above, or leaned against it and split from the side. Side-splitting is often more effective when the log does not have a flat top, or when you cannot stand it upright.

Always side-split a log or a half-split log that is leaning against another. Never split it from the end with your foot braced against the bottom. The upper end of the work must rest directly on the supporting log, and must not overhang it. Work from the opposite side of the supporting log, and be careful to strike the work at or below the point of support. Failure to observe these cautions can set the work catapulting toward your face.

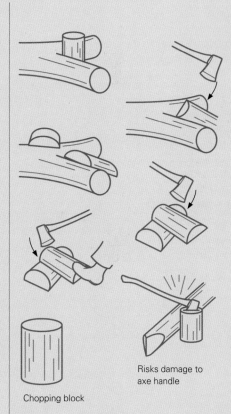

Chopping block

Risks damage to axe handle

1 SPLITTING LOGS

Wedges are required to split a log lengthwise. Although any wood will do, hardwood makes the best wedges. Make them about as long as the log's diameter, with an angle between 15 and 30°. Count on placing one every foot (30cm) or so. Make extras to allow for breakage or a tougher log.

You must start the split with an axe to make room for the wedge. Chop a narrow groove along the log's length. Then strike the axe hard into the groove at the end of the log, leaving the edge embedded in the wood. Use a hefty stick as a mallet against the poll to drive it in further. This should begin to open up the split large enough to insert the wedge. Remove the axe and repeat the process a foot (30cm) or less down the groove.

When wedges are in place along the length of the log, use the poll of your axe to tap them in further. Give just a few light taps to each before moving on to the next. Go back to the beginning and repeat, opening up the split bit by bit. If the point of a wedge gets dull and can't be driven further, place one immediately beside it and continue as usual. When the gap has widened sufficiently with the replacement wedge, you can easily draw out the damaged one to resharpen it.

SPLITTING SMALL STICKS

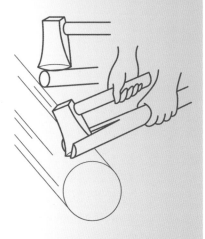

To split sticks that are too small to strike accurately, hold the work in your off hand right against the blade of the axe, pressing the edge firmly into the side of the stick, aligned with the grain. Keeping the two in contact, swing them together against the chopping surface.

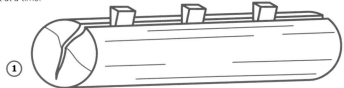

Large logs can be split with wedges. Use many of them, and tap each in a bit at a time.

①

Here are some tips for splitting large blocks of wood, gleaned from Mors Kochanski's *Bushcraft*:

- Cutting narrow slabs off the sides may be easier than splitting a large piece in half. This is especially true when using a hatchet.
- Cut from the crown toward the butt (top to bottom as the tree grows).
- Cut either parallel or perpendicular to the growth rings, not at any other angle to them.
- Strike the block with the toe of the blade, letting the heel overhang the edge of the work.
- If splitting perpendicular to the growth rings, set the axe firmly in the block, then turn them over together and swing so that the butt of the axe strikes the chopping surface. The large block will have more momentum than you can exert by swinging the axe.

2 HEWING

Hewing the top of a log flat will save you time in the construction of a dugout canoe.

The surface that will be the top of the canoe should face sideways. Block the log off the ground, using poles as levers. Make vertical charcoal marks at both ends of the log to define the upper edge of the hull.

Use your axe to make a small split where the coal mark meets the surface of the log, and insert a twig in the split. Do the same at the opposite end. Take a string and rub it against the charcoal to make a mason's "chalk line." Stretch it between the two pegs, then "snap" a straight line between them to define the sheerline. Remove the string and pegs. If you have sufficient clearance below the log, do the same to define the opposite sheerline.

About a foot (30cm) in from one end of the log, score straight down across the surface to connect the two sheerline marks. Repeat this every foot or two (30–60cm). With the edge of the axe aligned with the grain of wood, slab out the wood between the scores. Do not swing the axe as if you were chopping wood. Rather, move your dominant hand up the handle and keep it there, making the strokes straight down and keeping the handle horizontal. You should wear leather gloves and proceed with caution.

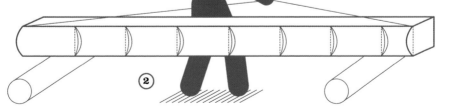

Use a charcoal-blackened string to line out your hewing cuts, then make vertical cuts of the proper depth at regular intervals before hewing the side down.

FIRST AID

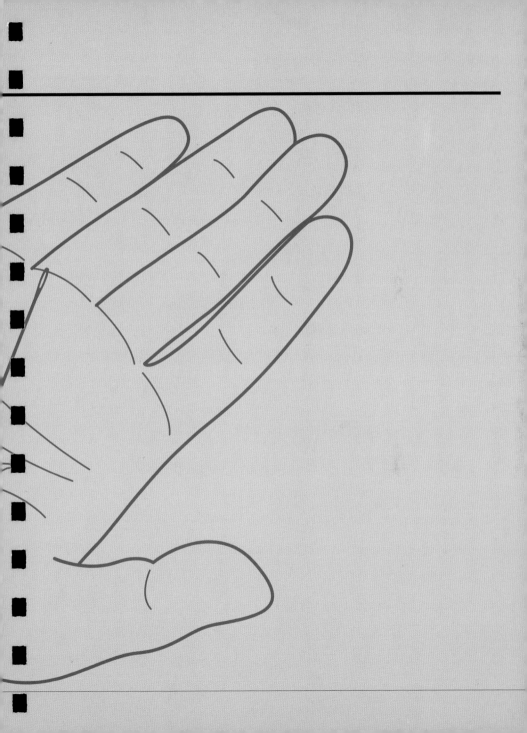

COMMON KNIFE AND AXE INJURIES

Everyone, regardless of whether they travel in the wilderness or ever pick up an axe, should know first aid. Life's hazards are so frequent and unpredictable that everyone should be capable of helping themselves or others in the case of common accidents and illnesses. This is stuff that every Boy Scout learns in his first few weeks, and you can too. Once you know it, you'll be amazed at the confidence it confers and how often you use it.

CUTS

Careless use of a knife or axe often results in "clean" cuts—in the sense that the skin or flesh is severed smoothly, not torn or ragged. But so-called clean cuts may be very dirty in terms of infection-causing bacteria, including the one that causes tetanus. In many cases, infection is the greater danger. Lacerations from edge tools may be superficial or deep, the latter cutting through skin and, potentially, muscle, tendons, and blood vessels. Lacerations may also be caused by sharp edges or points on the workpiece, which usually occur when the workpiece is improperly secured. These wounds are often ragged.

Stab wounds often occur when the knife slips while incautiously using the off hand to hold a workpiece. Stab wounds elsewhere on the body are often the result of falling on an unprotected knife, or against the sharp end of a cut-off limb on a tree. Like lacerations, puncture wounds may be shallow or deep and may involve tendons, blood vessels, and other organs.

FIRST AID DEFINED

According to Wikipedia, first aid is "...usually performed by non-expert, but trained personnel to a sick or injured person until definitive medical treatment can be accessed.... It generally consists of a series of simple and in some cases, potentially life saving techniques that an individual can be trained to perform with minimal equipment."

See pages 180–182 for information on treating cuts.

STRAINS AND SPRAINS

A strain is the excessive stretching or tearing of muscles or tendons—the fibrous bands that connect muscles to bones. Sometimes called a pulled muscle, a strain causes extreme soreness and impaired use of the muscles or limbs involved. Tendinitis is a specific type of strain: a tear in a tendon. Strains are most likely to occur when doing hard physical work to which you are not accustomed, such as chopping wood or lifting heavy loads. Stretching and warming up cold muscles before work can help to prevent this.

A sprain is the over-stretching or tearing of ligaments, the fibrous bands that connect bones to each other at the joints. Sprains are usually caused by a sudden wrench or jerk when a joint is bent or twisted beyond its limits, as could occur when losing control of a heavy log. In severe cases, it can cause permanent injury if not treated.

Treatment

First-aid treatment is the same for strains and sprains. The therapy regime, consisting of rest, ice, compression, and elevation, is known by the acronym "RICE."

- Rest: stop using the sprained or strained muscles or joints, using a sling or a splint if necessary to immobilize them.
- Ice: apply for 20 minutes every hour to reduce swelling and soreness. If ice is not available, cool the area with a cold-water compress.
- Compress: wrap an elastic bandage around the area. Do not wrap it so tightly as to restrict blood circulation.
- Elevate: raise the affected area above the heart.

EYE INJURIES

When chopping wood, flying wood chips or splinters may enter the eyes, resulting in irritation, laceration, or penetration. Implications for these injuries range from temporary discomfort to permanent loss of sight. Falling twigs present a danger when looking up while felling a tree. Wearing eye protection is the best means of avoidance.

Treatment

If you have something in your eye, do not rub or apply pressure to it. Wash your hands before touching your eye. Remove contact lenses if present. If a small object is over the cornea (the colored portion) or the pupil (the black center), use clean water to flush it out. If the object is over the sclera (the white part), touch it with a cotton swap or the corner of a tissue. The object will probably cling to it. In both cases, some irritation may persist for a day or more. Never use tweezers, a toothpick, or other hard object to remove something from the eye.

There are no practical first-aid treatments for more serious eye injuries such as scratches, lacerations, or embedded objects, other than the application of saline eyedrops, which may soothe the pain. Your response must be to seek professional medical attention promptly. In the meantime, keep the eye covered with dark glasses or a loose bandage that does not press on the eye.

BLISTERS

Hard work with soft hands can cause blisters—raised areas on the skin filled with lymph fluid. Anyone working with a knife or axe risks blisters from repeated friction and irritation of the skin by the handle of the tool. Blisters are uncomfortable and interfere with your ability to use the affected hand. Although not serious in and of themselves, they can become a site of infection when they break. Work gloves will often inhibit their occurrence.

Treatment

Small, unbroken blisters generally recede in a day or two and require no treatment. Avoid breaking them. Covering them loosely with a bandage may provide protection against breakage.

Large blisters are more prone to breaking. To avoid infection, treat a broken blister like any other open skin wound. (See page 182.)

If a large blister interferes with your ability to move comfortably, you may drain it. Clean your hands and the blister thoroughly, then sterilize a needle with rubbing alcohol. Puncture the blister near its edge and press the fluid out with your fingers. Wash it again, apply antibiotic ointment, and cover with a sterile dressing, changing it daily or whenever it gets wet or dirty. Do not cut away the loose skin.

DRAINING A BLISTER

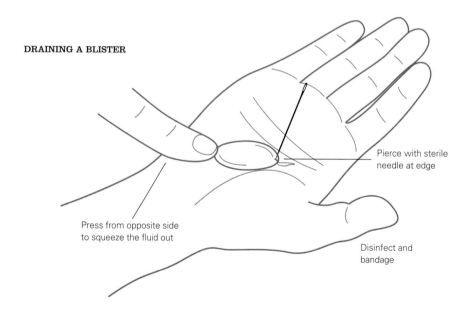

Pierce with sterile needle at edge

Press from opposite side to squeeze the fluid out

Disinfect and bandage

FRACTURES

Broken bones may be caused by inadequate axe control or lack of caution when felling trees or working on heavy timbers. Fractures may be "simple" (or "closed"), in which the skin remains intact, or "compound" (also "open"), in which the broken end bone punctures the skin and is exposed to the air. A "greenstick" fracture is one in which the bone is cracked but its pieces remain attached, while in a comminuted fracture, the bone is shattered into several pieces.

Treatment

Do not attempt to set, or "reduce" a break. First aid consists of immobilizing the fracture, after which professional medical attention must be obtained. In the case of a compound fracture, it is necessary to stop the bleeding and protect the open wound from infection. (See pages 180–182.)

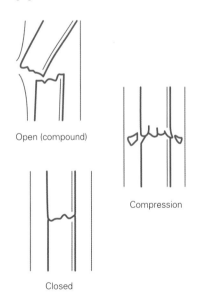

Open (compound)

Compression

Closed

CONCUSSION

Inadequate axe control may result in a rebound injury to the head, causing a concussion—a jarring injury to the brain. Another source of concussion danger is falling branches when felling a tree. Symptoms can include loss of consciousness, confusion, headache, nausea and vomiting, blurred vision, and impaired brain function. Damage may be minor or severe, temporary or permanent.

Treatment

Make the victim lie down and rest if he or she is conscious. Contrary to myth, you may let the victim sleep—it will not affect his or her ability to maintain or regain consciousness. Mild pain relievers such as aspirin or acetaminophen may be administered. If a lump forms on the head—a "goose egg" is caused by an accumulation of blood between the skull and the scalp—ice may be applied to reduce the swelling. Do not apply the ice directly: wrap it in cloth to avoid freezing the skin. If symptoms persist, seek medical attention.

SHOCK

Any injury may be accompanied by shock, a potentially life-threatening condition in which vital organs do not receive sufficient blood circulation. Symptoms include loss of consciousness, dizziness, extreme weakness, trouble standing, and loss of alertness.

Treatment

Lie the victim on his back and elevate his legs at least 12" (30cm). If the victim vomits, roll him on this side and allow the fluid to drain. Clear the throat if necessary with your finger. Keep the victim warm, but not uncomfortably hot. If the weather is very hot, cool the victim gently. Seek medical attention.

TREATING CUTS

See pages 176–177 for an introduction to knife and axe cuts and related injuries. For obvious reasons, cuts are the most common edge-tool injuries and, while most are mere inconveniences, some are life-threatening. Even small cuts present a risk of infection, which can turn a minor injury into a grave danger. In a survival situation where medical help is not readily available, it is essential to take all cuts seriously.

STOP THE BLEEDING

Steady direct pressure will stop the bleeding from most wounds. Except in extreme cases, where a delay of seconds might result in a dangerous loss of blood, take a few moments to minimize the chance of infecting the wound, thereby protecting yourself from possible blood-borne illnesses. Wash your hands with soap and water. If medical gloves are not available, use several layers of clean cloth, plastic bags or any other type of clean material.

Have the victim lie down and elevate the injured part above his heart, or do it for him if he is unable. Remove any visible objects that you can simply pick out of the wound, but do not take time yet to clean it. Remove or cut away clothing that obstructs the wound. Remove any jewelry like rings or bracelets that might get stuck if the area around the wound swells.

Apply direct, steady pressure to the wound for at least 15 minutes. If the bandage or cloth soaks through, place another one on top of it and reapply pressure as quickly as possible. Don't lift the bandage to look at the

A THREE-STEP PROCESS

First aid for cuts involves three steps:

1. Stop the bleeding.
2. Clean and treat the wound.
3. Dress the wound.

Suturing (stitching) a wound falls outside the realm of first aid and should only be done by medical professionals with adequate equipment and facilities.

progress—just keep the pressure on for a full quarter-hour by the clock, minimum.

Most wounds will stop bleeding or reduce to a trickle in 15 minutes, but may continue seeping for up to 45 minutes.

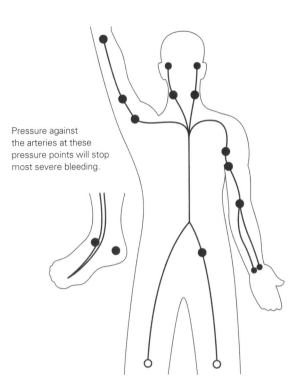

Pressure against the arteries at these pressure points will stop most severe bleeding.

PRESSURE POINTS

Victims of severe injuries such as amputated or crushed limbs could lose a quart (1 liter) of blood in a matter of minutes or seconds. Death will not be far behind. If direct pressure and elevation cannot stop this massive bleeding, constrict the affected artery at the pressure point closest "upstream" from the wound (i.e., nearer to the heart).

Pressure points are places where arteries are close enough to the skin so that pressure on them will close off the flow of blood. These include the location of the pulse in the wrist, the femoral artery on the inside of the thigh, and the carotid artery in the neck. Because constricting the artery closes off the flow of blood, tissue and organs downstream of the constriction are at risk of dying, so the procedure must be practiced only in extreme cases. Maintain pressure on a pressure point for a maximum of 10 minutes, then see if direct pressure will succeed in slowing the bleeding.

CLEAN AND DISINFECT THE WOUND

When bleeding has stopped, wash the wound with soap and water. Hydrogen peroxide does a good job loosening encrusted blood, but it is not an effective antiseptic. If the cut has left a flap of skin, lift it gently and irrigate it to flush out all visible debris. Use saline solution in a squeeze bottle, if available, as this does a good job of eliminating bacteria. Do not cut the flap off.

Apply an antibiotic ointment such as bacitracin to the outside of the wound to reduce the chance of post-injury infection. Tincture of iodine and mercurochrome are no longer recommended as antibiotics.

DRESS THE WOUND

Wounds must be covered with a bandage and kept clean and dry to minimize the chance of infection. It is a dangerous myth that wounds should be left exposed to the air. Air has no curative powers for wounds, but it does provide a medium for the introduction of potentially infectious bacteria.

Apply antibiotic ointment directly to the bandage and place it against the wound. Apply tape over the bandage, sticking it to the skin and avoiding the wound itself. Change the dressing at least daily, and whenever it becomes wet or dirty.

Do not attempt to suture a wound without proper training and adequate facilities. If sutures are necessary, keep the wound bandaged and immobilized to prevent it from opening up, and evacuate the victim as soon as possible.

AVULSIONS AND FLAPS

An avulsion is a cut in which the blade contacts the skin at a shallow angle and cuts or tears off a section of skin and, possibly, tissue. A flap is a partial avulsion, in which the cut tissue remains attached at one edge.

TOURNIQUETS

We mention tourniquets only because they are so well known, but we do not recommend their use. Because they cut off all circulation to the affected arm or leg, they are extremely dangerous to apply, and many health professional consider them an option of last resort. (In some jurisdictions, the use of a tourniquet by a lay person may be construed as practicing medicine without a license and may make the individual liable for injuries caused.) The use of pressure points is generally as effective at stopping severe bleeding, and far safer.

Compared to lacerations and puncture wounds, avulsions are easy to cleanse, because the entire injured area is exposed. But that exposed tissue is that much more prone to becoming infected until it is disinfected and dressed. A clean avulsion will generally take longer to heal than a clean laceration, and there is a constant risk of infection until new skin grows over the wound. Proper wound care—keeping it clean and dry, and changing the dressing frequently—is essential.

The wound beneath a flap can be particularly difficult to cleanse unless a syringe is available with which to inject sterile water or saline solution under pressure. If sufficient blood vessels are intact, the flap may survive and heal right over the wound, so don't cut it off. If it turns black, it will not survive, but it is not likely to cause infection by itself. Just allow it to dry up and fall off naturally. If the wound beneath a flap turns red, indicating infection, lift the edge of the flap to promote drainage of pus.

RESOURCES

BOOKS

Adney, Edwin Tappan and Howard I. Chapelle, *The Bark Canoes and Skin Boats of North America*. Smithsonian Institution Press, Washington DC, 1983

Elbroch, Mark and Mike Pewtherer, *Wilderness Survival: Living off the Land with the Clothes on Your Back and the Knife on Your Belt*. Ragged Mountain Press/McGraw-Hill, Camden, 2006

Gill, Paul G. Jr., MD, *Pocket Guide to Wilderness Medicine & First-Aid*. Ragged Mountain Press/McGraw-Hill, Camden, 1997

Johnson, Richard, *Rich Johnson's Guide to Wilderness Survival*. McGraw-Hill, New York, 2008

Kochanski, Mors, *Bushcraft: Outdoor Skills and Wilderness Survival*. Lone Pine Publishing. Edmonton, 1987

Paul, Don, *Everybody's Knife Bible: All new ways to use and enjoy your knives in the great outdoors*, 3rd ed. Path Finder Publications, Woodland CA, 1991

Pewtherer, Michael, *Wilderness Survival Handbook: Primitive Skills for Short-Term Survival and Long-Term Comfort*. McGraw-Hill, New York, 2010

Spielman, Patrick, *Sharpening Basics*. Sterling Publishing, New York, 1991

WEBSITES

Weisgerber, Bernie, author and Brian Vachowski, Project Leader. *An Ax to Grind: A Practical Ax Manual*. USDA Forest Service, Technology and Development Center, Missoula: http://www.fhwa.dot.gov/environment/fspubs/99232823/index.htm

American Knife & Tool Institute. http://www.akti.org/

Blade Forums: *The Leading Edge of Knife Discussion*. http://www.bladeforums.com/forums/content.php

Forest Applications Training: Tim's Tips. http://www.forestapps.com/tips/tips.htm

Knife Depot (Online retailer has worthwhile articles under the heading "Knife Info & Tips"). http://www.knife-depot.com/

Logging Safety: A Field Guide. http://www.health.state.ny.us/publications/3132/

Sharpening Made Easy: Knife Sharpening Information and Equipment. http://sharpeningmadeeasy.com/index.htm

Survival Topics: Your Online Survival Kit. http://www.survivaltopics.com/

Wilderness Survival. http://www.wilderness-survival.net/

Wild Food: Learn about edible and medicinal wild plants and mushrooms, nature, and ecology. http://www.wildmanstevebrill.com

Wilderness Survival Skills for safe wilderness travel. http://www.wilderness-survival-skills.com/

Wildfoods.info. http://www.wildfoods.info/index.html

Wildwood Survival. http://www.wildwoodsurvival.com/index.html

Woodcraft Wanderings. http://www.woodcraftwanderings.org/

GLOSSARY

amidships: the center of a boat, either front-to-back or side-to-side

back: the blunt side of a knife blade, opposite the edge. Also: spine

backcut: when felling, the cut made to a tree trunk on the side opposite to which it is intended to fall

baton: a club used to strike the spine of a knife blade. Also: to use a club in this manner

belt folder: a folding knife intended to be carried in a sheath

bit: the sharp end of an axe head; its edge

blood groove: a long recessed area on the side of a knife blade

bow: the front end of a boat

buck: to chop a log into sections

butt: the end of the handle on a fixed-blade knife or axe; also called the pommel on a knife

camp axe: a short two-handed axe with a handle about 2' (60cm) long

choil: the unsharpened section of a knife's blade next to the guard

chop: to cut through wood across the grain

clip point: a blade pattern in which the spine is cut to a concave profile near the point

deadfall: a trap that uses a deadweight to crush the prey

dominant (hand or side): the hand most used for work (e.g., the right hand of a right-handed person); the side of the body on that side

drop point: a blade pattern in which the edge curves up and the spine curves down to meet at the point

edge: the sharp side of a blade

fell: to chop down a tree. Also: fall

fixed-blade knife: a knife with no moving parts

flute: a flat or hollow area near the base of a spear or arrow point where the shaft is attached. Also: to form a flute

fuel wood: large sticks and logs upon which a fire feeds

gorge: a device tied to the end of a fishing line and intended to lodge in a fish's throat when swallowed

grind: the part of a knife blade that is ground to create the edge. Also: the cross-sectional shape of the ground edge, as in hollow-grind or flat-grind

grip: the handle on a fixed-blade knife

guard: a cross-piece separating the handle from the blade on a fixed-blade knife. Also: quillon

gunwale: a strengthening timber at the top edge of a boat's side. It may be an inwale, an outwale, or both.

gut hook: a small-diameter concave blade used in skinning and cutting through tendons

haft: an axe or knife handle. Also: to affix a handle to an axe or knife blade

handle: on a fixed-blade knife, the grip. On a folding knife, the pieces that make up the outside surfaces of the case, also known as the covers

hatchet: a one-handed axe. Also: hand axe

heel: the lower corner of an axe's edge

hinge: a portion of a tree trunk not cut when felling, between the undercut and the backcut, and essential to controlling the direction of the tree's fall

hone: to sharpen a blade

inwale: a strengthening timber at the inside top edge of a boat's side. See also gunwale

kindling: the lightest, finest flammable material used to start a fire

knife hand: see "on" hand

knob: the end of an axe handle. See butt

limb: to cut limbs from a tree

lockback: a folding knife with a mechanism to lock the blade in the open position

master blade: the largest blade on a pocket knife with multiple blades

multi-tool: a folding tool incorporating multiple implements, almost always including a knife blade

nail mark: a notch near the top of a folding blade into which a fingernail is inserted, to lift the blade from the case

nock: a notch in the end of a stick. Also: to fit an arrow onto a bowstring

"off" (hand or side): the hand not holding the knife, or the side of the body on that side

oil stone: a sharpening stone that uses oil as a lubricant

"on" (hand or side): the hand holding the knife, or the side of the body on that side

outrigger: a float held away from the side of a boat by poles, used as a stability aid. Also: a canoe so outfitted

outwale: a strengthening timber at the outside top edge of a boat's side. See also gunwale

pocket knife: a small folding knife intended to be carried in a trouser pocket

point: the tip of a blade

poll: the blunt end of an axe head

pommel: the butt of a fixed-blade knife

quillon: *see* guard

quinzhee: a shelter built by hollowing a mound of snow

ricasso: the flat section of a knife's blade between the guard and the beginning of the sharpened edge

sheath knife: a fixed-blade knife

sheepsfoot: a blade pattern in which the spine curves down to meet the straight edge at the point

sheer, sheerline: the uppermost edge of a boat's sides when viewed in profile

snare: a trap that uses a noose to capture prey

spar: a pole used to support a sail, as a mast, yard or boom

spine: the blunt side of a blade, opposite the edge. Also: back

split: to cut through wood along the grain

stern: the back end of a boat

stone: a flat natural stone or synthetic abrasive block used to sharpen a blade

strop: a leather strap used to refine the sharpness of a knife edge. Also: to use a strop

tang: the part of a knife blade hidden within the grip (in the case of a fixed-blade knife) or case (in the case of a folding knife when open)

thwart: a cross-piece on a boat connecting the gunwales or serving as a seat

tinder: twigs, bark, small sticks, and other easily combustible materials heavier than kindling and used in starting a fire

toe: the upper corner of an axe's edge

tomahawk: a one-handed axe used as a weapon

top: to cut the top off a tree

trailing-point blade: a knife blade whose point curves up so far that there is no steel directly behind it

undercut: when felling, the cut made to a tree trunk on the side to which it is intended to fall

warp: the lengthwise strands of woven fabric

water stone: a sharpening stone that uses water as a lubricant

weir: a fish trap consisting of poles driven into the bottom of the water body, often with netting or other fabric between the poles

wikiup: a shelter consisting of thatching or other materials over a conical framework

withies: thin tree branches or shoots useful for lashing

woof: the cross-wise strands of woven fabric. Also: weft

INDEX

CREDITS

All illustrations	© Rehab Design
Cover (Knife):	© Roman Peregontsev | Dreamstime.com
Cover (Background)	© Konstantin Sutyagin | Dreamstime.com
12	© Tossi66 | Dreamstime.com
13 left	© Tyler Olson | Dreamstime.com
13 right	© Homiel | Dreamstime.com
14	© Gena96 | Dreamstime.com
16 left	© Kirill Polovnoy | Dreamstime.com
16 right	© Nicholas Krul | Dreamstime.com
17 top	© Elena Schweitzer | Dreamstime.com
17 left	© Vagrant83 | Dreamstime.com
21	© Elf666 | Dreamstime.com
22	© Prill Mediendesign & Fotografie
23 top	© Ken Backer | Dreamstime.com
23 bottom	© Constantin Opris | Dreamstime.com
24 top	© Sean Macdiarmid | Dreamstime.com
24 bottom	© Karam Miri | Dreamstime.com
25 top	© Martinzak | Dreamstime.com
25 bottom	© Susan Leggett | Dreamstime.com
26 top	© Elf666 | Dreamstime.com
26 bottom	© Robert Clay | Dreamstime.com
27 top	© Jovani Carlo Gorospe
27 bottom	© Dmytro Tkachuk | Dreamstime.com
28 left	© Rsooll | Dreamstime.com
31	© Stewart Hyman | Dreamstime.com
34	© Bigheado2 | Dreamstime.com
35	© Lecajun | Dreamstime.com
36 both	© bladetech.co.uk
37 top left	© Antoinettew | Dreamstime.com
37 top right	© Ed Endicott | Dreamstime.com
37 bottom left	© Owen Price
37 bottomh right	© bladetech.co.uk
41 top	© Sergey Yakovlev | Dreamstime.com

NOTES